Memorable Encounters

Other books by the author:

Here Today, Gone Tomorrow (2002), a memoir
Mr Wonderful Takes a Cruise (2004), a travel book (I)
Haven't We Been Here Before? (2007), a family involvement
Trewinnard: A Cornish History (2012), the author's home
Mr Wonderful Seeks Immortality (2014), a travel book (II)

Memorable Encounters

John Nott

PEN & SWORD
POLITICS

First published in Great Britain in 2018 by
Pen & Sword Politics
An imprint of
Pen & Sword Books Ltd
Yorkshire – Philadelphia

ISBN 978 1 52675 115 7

A CIP catalogue record for this book is
available from the British Library.

Printed and bound in the UK by TJ International Ltd, Padstow, Cornwall.

Pen & Sword Books Limited incorporates the imprints of Atlas, Archaeology,
Aviation, Discovery, Family History, Fiction, History, Maritime, Military,
Military Classics, Politics, Select, Transport, True Crime, Air World,
Frontline Publishing, Leo Cooper, Remember When, Seaforth Publishing,
The Praetorian Press, Wharncliffe Local History, Wharncliffe Transport,
Wharncliffe True Crime and White Owl.

For a complete list of Pen & Sword titles please contact

PEN & SWORD BOOKS LIMITED
47 Church Street, Barnsley, South Yorkshire, S70 2AS, England
E-mail: enquiries@pen-and-sword.co.uk
Website: www.pen-and-sword.co.uk

Or

PEN AND SWORD BOOKS
1950 Lawrence Rd, Havertown, PA 19083, USA
E-mail: Uspen-and-sword@casematepublishers.com
Website: www.penandswordbooks.com

This book of sketches about people I have known in my life is dedicated to my wife, Miloska, and to my nine grandchildren

Contents

Introduction

I have known all the people in this book, but not much connects them with each other except their integrity – that is why I chose them. None of them died young so they will all have borne the scars of life, whether it was as a participant in the Arctic convoys to Russia in 1943 (Admiral Terry Lewin), disgraceful treatment at the hands of the police (Field Marshal Dwin Bramall) or vicious abuse in politics (Margaret Thatcher).

Inevitably all will be forgot; in the end it is all 'dust to dust, ashes to ashes'. But while most people in the book are still remembered by their contemporaries, they should be remembered with advantages. We should feast our neighbours.

Margaret Thatcher once described me as having a very low boredom threshold; I fear it is true. That boredom threshold always made me restless to move on. As a consequence I went from one profession or activity to another and I met interesting people on the way. Good people.

I started in the Army after school, then Cambridge, the City, politics, business, farming and country pursuits. And the people in this book come from all these diverse fields. I am conscious that the list has rather a military slant, so I was anxious to civilize it with a scientist (Martin Rees), a farmer (Billy Collins) and a poet (Ted Hughes).

This is not a memoir, so I regret that there is rather too much about me in the book; much of it is autobiographical. I did not set out to write a series of potted biographies. After all, many of those in this book have merited major biographies already. To celebrate the lives and achievements of my subjects, I have had to describe the circumstances and environment in which I met them. I have ranged quite widely with my comments on the issues which, I think, are relevant to each of my subjects. These views are mine, not theirs.

I think it is relevant to describe myself as a war child, not in the sense that I ever encountered the terrible traumas of today's young victims in the Middle East and Africa, but the coming of the war in 1939 when I was seven years old marked my life.

In the 1930s we lived a comfortable existence on the outskirts of London, from where my father commuted daily to his job in the City. I think we lived a life of what might be described as bourgeois gentility – we were not rich but we had servants – and I had a succession of nannies who were instructed to pour cod liver oil down my throat. This led to violent contests, good training for Cabinet government under Mrs Thatcher.

In 1939 I was sent to my Devon grandparents as an evacuee. I remember sitting in their drawing room when Neville Chamberlain announced on the wireless that we were at war: it was 3 September 1939. Tears poured down my grandmother's face; I did not wholly understand, but it was just over twenty years since the horrors of the First World War.

I would like to have included a sketch of my Victorian grandparents, but it was so long ago. They were very austere. It was a serious offence to leave a light on in an empty room. We are told that HM The Queen is quite austere herself and roams around Buckingham Palace turning off the lights. She must have learned this practice from my grandfather.

We were also instructed by the wartime authorities to save the valuable coal reserves of the country by limiting hot water in the bath to six inches. My grandfather painted a line around the bath to enforce this edict. I have not stayed at Buckingham Palace so I am unaware whether this practice has been extended there.

I conclude this brief mention of my grandfather by saying that, as a surgeon, he was one of four doctors in Bideford Hospital. It has been replaced by more than sixty doctors in the North Devon District Hospital in Barnstaple. Are we more healthy nowadays? Maybe so. My grandfather treated the poorer locals in the fishing village of Appledore for no charge; there was no National Health Service. Before antibiotics his favourite medicine was rhubarb and soda as he believed that constipation was the cause of most illness. His patients were reluctant to return for a repeat prescription. Hey presto. There was no queue to see a GP in wartime England.

My father was away at the war and my mother found it something of a strain living with her parents, so we moved to a cottage nearby in Northam, where my mother had been christened and married. It was fine there, although finding enough food was something of a problem. The ration books afforded each person two eggs, half a packet of butter (four ounces), four ounces of raw bacon and twelve ounces of sugar each week; children got extra milk, blackcurrant juice and rosehip syrup. Lord Woolton, the Minister of Food, praised the value of potato pie on the radio, and the recipe was circulated widely.

After being uprooted from London I was quite lonely and became rather introverted, for I had no friends. It is much the same today. I should have gone to the village school, but my father insisted from afar that I should go to a boarding prep school at the age of eight, which brings me to a schoolmaster (Douglas Shilcock).

My grandfather became my surrogate father and his interests were transformative for me. He was a true countryman, passionately interested in nature and country life. He had been brought up on Dartmoor, where his father had been a parson in the same village church for nearly fifty years. He was a keen fisherman, and an avid collector of butterflies and birds' eggs, activities both now banned. There were so many butterflies and songbirds in those days, unlike today. His favourite pastime was finding dormice: he should have had a dormouse on his coat of arms. Because he was a doctor, we had that rare instrument, a car. He took me everywhere. I include a West Country conservationist and fisherman in the book (Michael Charleston).

I had to decide whether to take my subjects in historical order, but decided not to. So my first subject is a brilliant, extraordinary and controversial character, Enoch Powell.

Chapter One

Enoch Powell

Politician

I was one of the congregation awaiting the arrival of Enoch Powell's coffin at his funeral in St Margaret's Westminster when my neighbour, Ronnie Grierson, whom I had known in the City firm of Warburg, said in a loud whisper, startling our surrounding mourners, 'I suppose you know, he is being buried in his uniform.' As the bearers moved down the aisle a respectful silence fell upon the crowded congregation. Powell had been a controversial figure right up until his death, mainly as a result of one foolish speech.

After the funeral Powell's body was taken up to Warwick where he was indeed buried in his brigadier's uniform among the soldiers of the Royal Warwickshire Regiment in which he had served, initially as a private soldier. He was really rather a strange man: when asked in April 1986 what he would like to be remembered for, he replied, 'I would like to have been killed in the war.'

He was the son of elementary school teachers, and his mother, who was the most important influence in his life, was the daughter of a policeman. The family, from Nonconformist stock in Wales, was ambitious and concerned with self-improvement.

Enoch won a scholarship to King Edward's School in Birmingham, which he entered in 1928 at the age of thirteen. There he was remembered as a loner and this fixed his character for the rest of his life. He was austere and did not make friends easily. Indeed, he was given the nickname 'Scowly Powelly', and a contemporary said of him, 'He could not smile and had a crocodile face of such ferocity that even the naughtiest boys were not prepared to tease him.' He was two years ahead of his contemporaries in study and when he took the Higher School Certificate, the equivalent of A-levels, he went into the examination having memorized in Greek the whole of St Paul's Epistle to the Galatians.

When he took the scholarship exam in Classics to Trinity College, Cambridge, he left the exam halfway through the allocated time and did two version of the same piece, one in the style of Thucydides and another in the style of Herodotus. At Trinity the Master of his college invited him to tea with other freshmen and, uniquely, he refused, saying, 'Thank you very much, but I came here to work.' By all reports he sat in his unheated room in an overcoat with a blanket across his knees working at the Classics. When he travelled – he was a traveller all his life – he often slept in Cambridge railway station. He set a standard for reclusiveness, politely refusing invitations because they interfered with his studies.

In 1931 he first met the poet A. E. Housman, then Kennedy Professor of Latin, on a staircase in Trinity; the author of 'A Shropshire Lad', Housman became Enoch's hero, but the friendship took years to develop. To an extent Powell modelled himself on Housman. He read and eventually wrote poetry with the same intensity. Neither Powell nor Housman was able to communicate easily with the outside world.

In 1934 Powell was elected a fellow of Trinity, specializing in the works of Thucydides and Herodotus, but he described himself as 'suffocating' in the enclosed world of the college. Every time he walked through its Great Gate, he said, '[I] felt that I was going out of this world into something enclosed and all my instincts were to get out of what was enclosed in this world.' I felt the same myself as an undergraduate at Trinity.

In due course he accepted an appointment as Professor of Greek at Sydney University, where in the 1930s he developed increasing frustration and anger at the appeasement of Hitler and saw Munich as a disgrace. He went around saying, 'We want war', which must have surprised Australians on the other side of the world. It was at this time that he developed an obsession about being killed. He wanted to die in the front line, but this privilege was always denied him; he was to become the most senior intelligence officer in India, and then the youngest brigadier in the British Army.

In the years immediately before the outbreak of the war he returned to Europe, spending time in Germany, where he was briefly arrested by the Gestapo. He spoke German fluently (as well as six other languages) and was a passionate follower of Nietzsche. He then went on to Russia, learned Russian, and came to believe that Britain's long-term future lay in an alliance with Russia against the Americans. His dislike and suspicion of America and the Americans, which he maintained quite discreetly all his life, was one of the few prejudices he shared with Edward Heath.

That brings me back to Enoch's funeral. He was intensely proud of having been recruited into the Royal Warwickshire Regiment as a private soldier. He only managed this, at a time in the Phoney War in 1940, by posing as a Commonwealth citizen from Australia. He said that the most honourable and testing promotion that he ever received in life was from private to lance corporal.

In India during the war, as a brigadier in intelligence, his requests to join the front line in Burma being always denied, he prepared the plan for the country's defence in post-war days. In fulfilment of this task he travelled all over India and developed a great passion for the Raj. He fell deeply in love with India and the Indians, so much so that he developed an ambition to become Viceroy, one he realized could only be achieved through the English political system.

As may be imagined, he pored over that outstanding novel *A Passage to India* by E. M. Forster and said, after Attlee had agreed to Indian independence – the idea of which horrified him – 'The dream that the British and the Indians dreamed together for so long, a dream unique in human history in its strangeness and improbability, was bound to break one day. Even India, the land of hallucinations, could not preserve it forever from its contradictions.'

This was Enoch at his emotional best, expressing his sorrow at the ways of politics; in spite of his set of strong beliefs and principles, he was always prepared to accept the inevitability of change and the need for adaptability.

On demobilization, Enoch found his way into politics with the future of India at the forefront of his mind. The story goes that an official once told Winston Churchill that he might like to read Brigadier Powell's report on the recovery and defence of India. Churchill is said to have replied that he did not have the time to see that 'madman', and, indeed, the sense among the Macmillan generation that somehow Powell was mad was prevalent. He was always lecturing his colleagues with views, particularly on economic issues, which were outside the accepted conventions of the time.

Although I never came to understand Enoch, I share his view that soldiering and politics are the two professions that all men should aspire to. By soldiering Enoch was thinking of the life of a private soldier not a general; and in politics, of a parliamentarian not a Minister. Although he admitted that he would like to hold high office one day, he was happy with the freedom of the backbenches which gave him untrammelled scope to explore the intellectual and practical limits of parliamentary democracy – and this is where his gift to our country's economic policy is so profound. 'I do not deny', he said, 'that I would like to have been Secretary of State for Defence, but that would have been at the price of renouncing my freedom to speak my mind on matters which seemed to me to be of transcending interest and importance.'

There were two reasons why I got to know Enoch rather better than most other parliamentary colleagues. He was always, of course, a brooding presence during my time as Economic Secretary in the Treasury. I often suffered from his biting tongue, particularly during the Heath government. I was the poor sod who day after day found himself defending Heath's economic policy in the House of Commons. I did not believe in it, but I saw no purpose in resigning. When Enoch had left the Conservative Party for the Ulster Unionists he gave me an easy time in Parliament throughout the Falklands campaign – and he supported my Defence Review in 1982.

But more particularly, I was one of the younger members of the One Nation Dining Club, which met weekly in the House of Commons to discuss topical, mainly economic, issues. Heath dropped out when he became leader of the Conservative Party, but other members of the Macmillan generation like Reginald Maudling, Robert Carr, Sir Keith Joseph, Iain Macleod and Enoch were regular attendees. There was a philosophical gulf between the Macmillanism, represented especially by Carr and Maudling, and the younger entrants to Parliament in 1964–6 who were seeking a complete break from Macmillan's paternalist, collectivist consensus and the 'politics of decline'. The weekly arguments, with Enoch mainly against the rest, were fascinating for a new member like myself.

The more important and instructive gathering was under the auspices of the Economic Dining Group. This was founded by Nicholas Ridley and John Biffen, two of Enoch's admirers: the idea was to try and anchor Powell in the Conservative Party. Ever since Heath had forced through the European Communities Act, Enoch had been threatening to leave the Conservative Party, which he did in 1974. Thereafter he came back to Parliament – but as an Ulster Unionist.

The meetings of the Economic Dining Club took place once a month in members' houses. The other members, apart from Ridley and Biffen, were John Eden, Jock Bruce-Gardyne, Michael Allison, Peter Hordern and Cranley Onslow. We had a debate about inviting new members, and Margaret Thatcher, who was leading the Opposition Treasury team in Parliament, was suggested, but she was vetoed 'because she talks too much'. When she became leader of the Party, she joined us and was an assiduous attendee each month. There, under a dominating Enoch Powell, we thrashed out the economic issues of the day – and due to Enoch more than any other person, what came to be known as Thatcherism saw its birth in our discussions.

Every issue discussed led to a forceful intervention by Enoch, who fastened on any inconsistency or flaw in other people's arguments. But he did so always, even in private society, with blazing eyes and a thin smile. My wife, busy serving the meal on one occasion, said something about 'principles'. 'Principle, principle, principle,' said Enoch in a questioning way. To this day, we ponder what he meant, because he himself was a man of principle.

I remember an occasion when Hector Laing, who was a well-known establishment figure, chairman of his biscuit empire and a close friend of Margaret Thatcher, came to a meeting of Conservative backbenchers. He was appointed to the Court of the Bank of England. Clutching a prepared speech, he began, 'The days of unfettered capitalism are over . . .' These were the only words he had uttered, before Enoch, who was sitting in the front row, immediately stood up and shouted, 'Stick to biscuits', before walking out of the room and slamming the door as he went. The speed of Enoch's reaction was highly entertaining, but not for Sir Hector, I suppose.

One evening we dined in some private club and the discussion went on very late. We found the exit door locked and had to climb out along a balcony and over a drainpipe. Nick Ridley's memoir captures the picture of Enoch climbing down the drainpipe in his blue overcoat and Homburg hat.

Enoch's was the most influential intellect of my generation. He certainly created the concept of Thatcherite economics which was adopted by Keith Joseph, Thatcher herself, and later followed by Tony Blair and succeeding governments. At the heart of his belief was the inviolability of markets – and in particular the price mechanism. In a democracy he believed that it was only through the price mechanisms that competing demands can be reconciled: 'To my own satisfaction I reached the conclusion that the price mechanism is one of the means by which a society takes certain collective decisions in a manner not necessarily ideal but in a manner which is manageable and acceptable and broadly speaking is regarded as workable, a mechanism which cannot safely or wisely be replaced by conscious formulation and by compulsion.' He believed that the early action of the first Thatcher government to abolish price and incomes legislation – and abolish exchange control – was the start back from Macmillan tri-partisanship and indicative planning on the French model so much admired by Edward Heath, Carr, Maudling and others.

Heath endorsed a memorandum to him as Prime Minister by Reginald Maudling which read:

> The job of the Treasury is to use the instruments at its command to make the real economy grow faster, thereby bringing down unemployment and delivering real wage increases, workers will restrain their real wage demands, and as they restore their share of rising output, inflation will fall.

Economists at this time talked about the 'real wage push theory'; it was utter nonsense and led to what was described as the 'Barber boom', the loss of the 1974 election and the chaos faced by the Callaghan administration, which tried but failed to keep the trades unions under proper control. The only way to discipline the trades unions was by means of monetary policy, adopted by the incoming Thatcher government.

In contrast to the Macmillan consensus and tri-partisanship I have to include a speech made by Enoch Powell at the Conservative Party conference in Brighton in 1964. It set out succinctly what to me is the foundation of all good economic policy making.

> There is no secret about the cause of the 'cycle of stagnation, restriction and debt'. For a quarter-century we have been taught to believe that our livelihood depends on a pretence, on pretending that a £ is worth more in the world than it is. So we cling desperately to a fixed exchange. But so long as the price of anything is fixed, it will nearly always be wrong: for everything in the real world is changing all the time. The result has been either a surplus or a deficit and increasingly often a deficit. So we borrowed huge sums to keep up the fiction and accepted government interference in our lives in all directions. Once you have a wrong price fixed for anything, there is no interference by government that cannot be justified.
>
> This being the cause, the remedy is plain. We have to do what we were on the verge of doing after 1951 but unhappily did not. We have to set the rate for the pound free to behave like any other price and keep supply and demand in balance. A fortnight ago this would have sounded like theory. For ten days now it has been fact. The pound has been floated, at least against the mark and, contrary to expectation, the world has not come to an end . . .
>
> The truth is better, the truth is safer; and the truth is freer. In this, as in so much besides today, our fears are our own worst enemy. Let us dare to face reality: it is the road to freedom.

Just think about it. In all those post-war years one government after another supported a fixed exchange rate for the pound. Devaluation became the number one dirty word in politics in spite of the fact that it became necessary in one exchange rate crisis after another. Every month the Treasury published the balance of payments statistics – and did its Treasury best to cook the figures. Yet the balance of payments didn't matter – what mattered was the price of the pound against other currencies.

I was involved in a great run on the pound in 1974 – although perhaps John Major's government suffered an equal humiliation for the country when it clung to a fixed rate in the ERM, losing billions across the exchanges. In 1974, it became impossible to hold the fixed rate of exchange. Tony Barber, the Chancellor, Ted Heath, myself as Economic Secretary and Treasury officials met in the Prime Minister's room in the House of Commons. Ted Heath, with his fixation on being a good member of the European club, was a great supporter of holding currencies fixed together, in a need for stability and as a step towards European Monetary Union. I give Heath full marks that he saw that, against all his instincts, the only way out was to float the pound, not devalue it. We did so, and, subject only to Major's incompetence with a fixed rate through the ERM a few years later, we have been floating ever since.

I don't want this sketch of Enoch Powell to descend into an economic seminar – that would be tedious for most readers – but I have to applaud Enoch's gift to our country: sanity in appreciating the essential nature of the price mechanism, only possible in free markets. We should remember three fundamental strategic facts. First, that the Americans could never have humiliated this country at Suez if we had been the possessors of a floating pound; the fixed rate of sterling enabled Macmillan, as Chancellor, to rat on his colleagues and force our surrender at Suez. Second, my belief that we could not have carried out the Falklands campaign had we been operating under a fixed rate of exchange; and third, that the collapse of the European Union is inevitable if it persists in the single currency, driving southern Europe into increasing poverty and unemployment; we could not possibly be part of it.

As I write, the Europe debate continues, following the Referendum, like 'weeds through concrete', to quote an Enoch phrase. In a sense he was a British Gaullist favouring a partnership of nation states. Enoch's principled opposition to the Rome Treaty led him to abandon the Conservatives for Labour in the 1974 election. Powell had long argued, some would say with keen judgement, that the logic of the Rome Treaty, for better or worse, would compel centralism. He could not believe or accept that the British Parliament would ever forego its right to make its own laws, be subject to a European court of justice and defer to a foreign bureaucracy based in Brussels. It was inconceivable to him that British patriots could ever relinquish their rights to govern themselves. The weeds are certainly coming through the concrete today as we negotiate our exit from the European Union which still dreams of centralism and control. Heath managed to force the European Communities Act through Parliament on a guillotine motion with a majority of seven. We never entered the Common Market with the full heartfelt consent of the British people.

It is inevitable that I finish with the 'Rivers of Blood' speech in Birmingham in April 1968. Tony Blair will only be remembered for Iraq, Major for the currency crisis as we were forced out of the ERM, Cameron for his Referendum and Enoch for his Birmingham speech on immigration. It is all very unfair, but that is politics.

Enoch's speech caused considerable distress among his friends, including John Biffen. The violence of his language was a great mistake. Ted Heath was right to dismiss him from the Shadow Cabinet. Powell himself excused it, just, saying that he should have emphasized the quotation marks around the statements made by others. Enoch was never a racist; it is an absurd charge. But in today's terms he certainly made a racist speech. He was arguing against the number and concentration of immigrants in some of our cities – which he believed would lead to unacceptable tensions and violence in society; so far he has been proved wrong, but if we examine the remarkable result of the EU Referendum it seems that immigration is still a toxic subject some fifty years later.

Chapter Two

Sir Siegmund Warburg

Banker

Warburgs is the story of two remarkable men, Siegmund Warburg and Henry Grunfeld, who changed the City of London in the 1960s and greatly contributed to its becoming the most important financial centre in the Western world.

Their creation was like a meteor that came out of nowhere and blazed its way into the empty, staid, complacent, gentlemanly City of the immediate post-war world, transforming it into a vibrant financial centre. It remains to this day the greatest contributor to the wealth of the United Kingdom. Then the Warburg meteor fizzled out and disappeared completely. It is no more; and I suspect that most of the middle-aged and younger generation of bankers have scarcely heard of it, nor would they accept or understand its heritage.

Siegmund Warburg and Henry Grunfeld were Jewish immigrants from Nazi Germany. Grunfeld had suffered several frightening encounters with the Gestapo right up to 1938, when he left Germany. Both made England their home, and they were eternally grateful to this country. But they were essentially German, and very un-English in their attitudes and behaviour.

The trauma that these two exiles suffered needs to be understood. Grunfeld, for example, used to leave home in the very early hours and walk in the London parks because he felt that the British police might round up former Germans for internment in the morning. This was a man who came from a successful and prominent family in the German metal business; it was expropriated by the Nazis.

The Jewish heritage is really too sad to contemplate.

Siegmund Warburg was a Jewish aristocrat, 'a nineteenth-century German trapped in twentieth-century England'. He was interested in literature, politics, philosophy and in managing people, especially his young men. He was at one stage the City's most prominent banker, but he never read a balance sheet and was not much interested in making money. He believed in relationship banking, not the transaction banking of today's American investment banks. He was essentially a consummate diplomat who would have prospered in an environment like the Austro-Hungarian Empire, bringing together warring factions and personalities into a consensus.

When he pretended to hand over the management and control of his firm to Henry Grunfeld he circulated a memorandum among the directors of the bank stating that his 'aim was for democratic unanimity rather than democratic leadership'. But this aim, he said, would run the risk of 'excessive parliamentarianism – and bureaucratic bottlenecks'. He wrote to Grunfeld:

> Since I transferred a large part of my responsibilities to you, it is necessary that you have the ultimate authority and share it with others only to the extent to which you consider it right and appropriate.

In fact, Henry Grunfeld had already been running the bank for years, but he pretended otherwise. Grunfeld was far and away the cleverest man I met in my lifetime, perhaps approached in brainpower only by Enoch Powell. He was everything that Siegmund was not: practical, clever, down-to-earth, very active and a complete master of financial detail.

I admired Siegmund Warburg, but I did not really like him. He was quite unstable and neurotic. I loved Henry Grunfeld, however. He was austere, controlled, dedicated, rather dull maybe, but undoubtedly a great man.

How come I have the right to make these judgements? At the bank I was like a Civil Service Private Secretary, a role that Warburg created for his young men. I sat in a room between Warburg and Grunfeld for an entire year – and when the two of them met for consultation, agreement and disagreement they tended to do so in my room. I will explain how I came to be an employee of the bank for some seven years after leaving

Cambridge, and it was from Warburgs at the age of thirty-four that I entered politics.

I was in my room at Trinity, Cambridge, wondering what to do next for my career. By chance I read an article in the *Observer* in 1956 about the struggle for the control of British Aluminium. It divided the City between what was then an upstart firm called Warburgs and the establishment banks like Lazard, Morgan Grenfell and Schroders; they resented Warburgs with its foreign ways. Warburgs won that contest thanks to Grunfeld's skill, and the City was never the same again. Its gentlemanly and complacent ways were undermined forever.

I don't think the City was anti-Semitic, but there was an underlying mistrust of Jewish bankers, although some of the great bankers of the past like the Rothschilds and Ernest Cassel, adviser to Edward VII, had made the City great in the period before the First World War. This suspicion of foreigners is beautifully exemplified by an internal Bank of England memorandum about Walter Salomon, whom I knew. He was rather a tiresome man:

> Mr Randell of the Bank of England says he is a very pushing individual – German Jew – who established himself here in 1938. They don't know a lot about him, but think it would do no harm to let him cool his heels a bit more . . . he knows all about foreign exchange business but 'they haven't caught him out yet' . . . His office is full of foreigners . . . Mr Bull [also of the Bank of England] quoted the old saying, 'I do not like you Dr Fell, the reason why I cannot tell'.

Anyhow, after reading about the Aluminium battle I wrote a letter directly to Siegmund Warburg asking for a job. My father was shocked. 'Warburg is certainly clever,' he wrote to me, 'but you know it's not the sort of firm where you should start your career.' To me it looked radical, anti-establishment and on the move. I liked the sound of it. I obtained a reply from Warburg personally almost by return, telling me that Ronald Grierson, whom I sat next to in later years at Enoch Powell's funeral, would call on me in my rooms at Cambridge. Grierson duly arrived and told me to arrange a visit to Mr Warburg in London, which I did.

Ronnie Grierson had been a German refugee and had enlisted as a private in the Pioneer Corps in order to avoid internment. He finished the Second World War as a lieutenant colonel in the Black Watch, having served all over Europe in the Special Operations Executive (SOE) and in the SAS.

'I am very flattered that you should want to join my firm,' said Mr Warburg. This was in 1959 when there were only two hundred or so employees – it rose to 6,500 in 1984, when it effectively collapsed.

He went on to say, 'I understand from Mr Grierson that you are about to become President of the Cambridge Union. I am surprised that you do not wish to enter politics.'

'Maybe I would like to do so one day,' I said, 'but I want to make a career first.'

'How interesting,' said Warburg. 'Well, someone who wants to go into politics is just the sort of person I'd like to have in my firm. You know, if I hadn't got a German accent I would certainly want to go into politics myself.'

Flattery was always Siegmund Warburg's weapon.

This episode illustrates how very different Warburgs was from every other firm. It is impossible to imagine any other bank wanting to recruit a would-be politician, or sending an immediate reply from the Chairman in answer to a job application from an undergraduate.

Warburgs was known for its eccentric employment policy and recruited people who would not have fitted comfortably into established City firms. Although most of my new colleagues had been to Oxbridge, Warburgs was ambivalent about English elite education and on occasion blamed Grierson's 'beastly public school education' for his allegedly 'unaggressive and unpugnacious spirit'. Martin Gordon, another colleague, had been around the route looking for a job, but all the other banks wanted to know was which school he had been to – and where his family came from.

Class was not the touchstone for recruitment at Warburgs. As Warburg himself explained in 1980, 'Those with whom I am close in my firm are people with whom I can also talk about books, about music, about human beings, human problems. If a fellow would come to me and say his interest is athletics, I think he would not stand a chance.'

He was highly resistant to the graduates of business schools and qualified economists: 'The young men who I think have the best future in banking, are, as a rule, those who during their educational period have been good classical scholars.'

When I became the Chairman of Lazard, another merchant bank, in later years, it used to irritate me that the younger directors always recruited clever Oxbridge graduates like themselves; I liked the spirit and ambition of young City traders but I had a problem getting them accepted into a stuffy City bank of clever public school boys.

Another habit among the German refugees whom we called 'the Uncles' was their determination to find a Jewish ancestor among their English colleagues. Ian Fraser, another clever recruit who spoke fluent German, was alleged by them to have Jewish blood. He was the grandson of Lord Lovat and his mother was the daughter of the Earl of Verulam! A frequent visitor was Sir Brian Mountain, the Chairman of the Eagle Star Insurance Company, and the Uncles were determined that he had changed his name from 'Berg – 'He talks of fishing and shooting as if to hide it.' No amount of explanation would convince them that he was of English stock.

The Uncles' German accents caused a certain amount of mirth among the members of the bank. Peter Stormonth Darling, who ran the investment department, told of his encounter with Mr Korner, a refugee from Austria. The conversation went as follows:

Korner:	Darling, I'm going on holiday next week, I am going to Essen.
Darling:	Mr Korner, you can't be going to Essen for a holiday, no one goes to Essen for a holiday.
Koener (impatiently):	No, Darling, not Essen. Essen.
Darling:	Why on earth do you want to go to Essen, Mr Korner?
Korner:	Not Essen – Essen – where zey have
(even more impatiently)	ze Parsenon [Parthenon].

Another holiday destination sounded to Darling as if it was Pakistan; it turned out to be Bad Gastein.

Enough of this frippery. Why do I claim that Warburg changed the City? After the British Aluminium battle, the bank became the choice of businesses to make an acquisition or fend off an unwanted raider. The established City firms saw a slow move of their best clients away to this more aggressive upstart. This practice became known as corporate finance, and within the period from 1960, when I joined the bank, into the 1980s it became the leader of restructuring and amalgamation in the City. Its rise to pre-eminence became unstoppable. Warburg personally became a closet adviser to Harold Wilson during his first period as Prime Minister. He courted the politicians of the day with acuity, and they were continual guests at Warburg lunches. Bernard Kelly, another member of the team, tells me that after a lunch with a prospective client he was asked to prepare an undated letter praising the intelligence and wisdom of the visitor, to be despatched with another invitation three months later.

The greatest triumph, however, was not so much Warburgs' skill in relationship banking, courting and retaining corporate clients, but in its creation of the Eurobond market, which restored the City to its pre-1914 pre-eminence as an international financial market. It all began in a very small way.

Siegmund Warburg's family, if not as famous as the Rothschilds, had established a considerable reputation as bankers in Germany and the United States. Siegmund's cousins and ancestors had created the leading German merchant bank in Hamburg in the 1870s, and his relations were founders of the Federal Reserve in America and were partners of the distinguished investment bank Kuhn Loeb on Wall Street. Siegmund played these contacts for all their worth and created a web of admirers, among them Hitler's associate Hermann Abs, the Chairman of Deutsche Bank.

When the American financial authorities became increasingly worried about the US balance of payments in the early 1960s they imposed controls on New York's international capital market which opened up a market in offshore dollar denominated bonds – now known as Eurobonds. Warburg grasped this opportunity and persuaded his friend Guido Carli, the governor of the Italian central bank, to issue a dollar denominated loan for Autostrada, the Italian motorway toll company. It was for $15 million and Deutsche Bank was a lead investor – a tiny start to what has become a huge international capital market running into billions.

I enjoyed many interesting experiences as Siegmund Warburg's personal assistant or bag carrier. He came into my room one day and said he was taking me to New York with his secretary, Doris Wasserman. 'Please come into my room, Nott, and I will speak to David Rockefeller, the Chairman of Chase Manhattan Bank.'

I listened in to the conversation.

'David, you are a very great man,' said Siegmund, 'I want your help. I am going to New York to try and sort out my relationships in Wall Street, and I wondered if you could offer me accommodation.'

David Rockefeller obliged without demur and said he would be delighted to welcome him.

So we arrived in New York and were given an entire floor of the Chase in Park Avenue for the three of us. Warburg then tried to disentangle himself from his partnership in Kuhn Loeb and replace it with a close relationship with Lehmans, in the 1960s the most prominent and active investment bank in Wall Street. I used to spend my days in Lehmans, then presided over by Robert Lehman, the senior partner.

'Can you show Nott around your art collection, Robert?' So Robert Lehman took me to his house to show me round, going from the top floor of Renaissance masterpieces to the Impressionists on the ground floor. His collection would later become a prized possession of the Metropolitan Museum.

Siegmund was always doing things like this for me. 'Nott, I want you to meet Kit Hoare. I have arranged for you to lunch there later in the week. Let me know what they discuss.' I was an unknown bag carrier; Kit Hoare was a major City figure.

With a Germanic passion for recording everything, all the incoming and outgoing letters and the memoranda of every meeting were circulated daily around the bank. Every comma and paragraph was open to comment by the Uncles.

Peter Stormonth Darling, in his outstanding book *City Cinderella* about the Warburg investment department, related an incident that took place on Christmas Day 1964. Just after noon, the telephone rang in his house. It was Warburg.

'I do hope I'm not disturbing you . . .'

'Oh no, Mr Warburg, not at all.'

'Well, it's about your note dated 22 December on the American stock market. Do you have it in front of you?'

'Er, no. I'm afraid my copy is in the office.'

'Well, let me remind you on the second sentence in the fifth paragraph. I think there should be a comma after the word "development".'

This was on Christmas Day!

Warburg was brilliant at creating a work ethic among his staff. He was lavish with praise when warranted, and silently hostile to any remarks which he regarded as negative or cynical. Young men in the City wanted to work there and felt that they were part of an exciting team. In many ways it was like a medieval court. People were in favour and then ignored. No one was dismissed because, when it became clear they were not wanted, by their own choice they quietly disappeared.

Warburg had a particular interest in the young men of the bank; he knew all of them and encouraged them with a paternal smile. It gave them confidence and status. It was an ongoing lesson in leadership.

With some reluctance, I have to draw a comparison with another banker. When I was Chairman of Lazard in London, a Frenchman, Michel David-Weill, was my principal shareholder. Like Warburg, David-Weill had all the charm and the inherited skill of several generations in merchant banking. He was highly respected in Wall Street for his great wealth, and I used to fly across in Concorde to see him frequently. But he believed that his team was motivated by money (a Wall Street vice). He paid great attention to his rainmakers – the men who brought in business – but he hardly knew, or was interested in, the junior members of the bank. He was an interesting and pleasant man, but not a leader, and when his top team could no longer earn the same as their peers in Goldman or Morgan Stanley, he could not hold them together. His greedy partners deserted him.

I said earlier that the Warburg meteor failed, and the bank no longer exists except as a subsidiary of a Swiss commercial bank. How did its collapse come about? I debate with my former colleagues what really happened.

Grunfeld was still around but Warburg himself went off to live in Switzerland and died in 1982. I last met Warburg outside Margaret

Thatcher's office in 1981. As I left her study, there he was, no doubt with some great scheme to put to the Prime Minister, whom he admired.

By that time, Big Bang had hit the City, and the partners of many distinguished firms like Rowe & Pitman sold out and joined American firms, or in this case Warburgs. The place became just another English institution.

English culture changed the ethos of a Jewish bank. Englishmen and English culture destroyed it. Foolishly, the new team set out to create an English competitor to the big investment banks in Wall Street. It failed. Costs were out of control, as evidenced by the vast number of people employed, against the 200 when I joined it. It was sold to the Swiss Bank Corporation for £850 million, a small amount beside the investment department – Mercury Asset Management – that sold to Merrill Lynch for £3.1 billion in 1997.

Would it have happened if Siegmund Warburg had still been around and Henry Grunfeld had been a younger man? I doubt it.

Warburg never liked the stock market. By necessity he dealt with senior stockbrokers, such as the admirable father of former Prime Minister David Cameron; but he had a disguised contempt for their profession. He thought markets were essentially casinos run by people without intellect – or long-term foresight. He believed in what he called 'haute banking', the creation of long-term relationships, not the transaction and trading so typified by the obsessed American investment banks. He would, I think, like Rothschilds, have stayed aloof from Big Bang. He would have tried to stay small, and would have nurtured his people with their personal talents and deficiencies.

Would it have been possible to hold his team together when young bankers were becoming rich in vulgar, big-bracket investment banks? And would the City have grown back into pre-1914 pre-eminence without the incursion of American attitudes and practices? Again, I doubt it. I acknowledge that the world moves on, and also acknowledge, reluctantly, that Big Bang was good for Britain, however much one may detest Wall Street, its greed and practices.

Chapter Three

Lord Lewin

Admiral of the Fleet

Terry Lewin, together with Martin Rees, is possibly the most interesting man I have met in my lifetime; that is not to say that Margaret Thatcher, Enoch Powell, Ted Hughes and others were not remarkable people. But it is the humility and quiet demeanour of the man which made him so very special.

He died relatively young, at seventy-eight, weighed down with all the honours our strange customs and ancient traditions require: Admiral of the Fleet, Distinguished Service Cross won on the Arctic convoys – that comes first, then Knight of the Garter and Order of the Bath. All these honours somehow diminished the man, because in the last resort he was a simple soul. In photographs I thought he looked out of place in his Garter robes and chains of office. He would have been great without any flummery, like many of our simple and unknown countrymen today.

I had the good fortune and privilege of knowing Terry Lewin well. By chance he was Chief of the Defence Staff throughout my time as Defence Secretary – it was also odd for a peaceful soul like me to find myself at war in the Falklands with an Admiral of the Fleet! So much of life is about chance, and all of us soldier on, making the best of where we find ourselves. I gave him a rotten time when I had to reduce the forward building programme of the Royal Navy, his greatest love. Unlike the Chief of Naval Staff, who went quite bonkers, Terry with his loyalty and personal prejudices pulling in all directions, remained calm throughout and particularly considerate with me, the alleged destroyer of the Royal Navy. The principal charge was that I reduced the number of frigates to fifty – it's now down to nineteen – but more of that later.

During the Falklands campaign I saw him daily and often more than that. I have failed on many occasions to make the right decisions in life but with Terry I got it right at the beginning of the campaign. Margaret Thatcher proposed that I should brief the War Cabinet during the war; I declined and said it would be better done by Lewin. At that stage she hardly knew him but agreed that it was appropriate. The relationship between Margaret and Lewin was unique and a winner; they trusted one another implicitly and formed the closest working relationship. The two of them together, from separate standpoints, won the Falklands War.

Let me begin, however, by considering the drama that accompanied my Defence Review in 1982 – Command 8288. Most of its critics, especially within the Royal Navy, have never understood it. We were always going to retain two aircraft carriers, the two assault ships and fifty frigates. The savings made in the forward programme, about £7 billion, came from closing Chatham and Gibraltar dockyards – and abolishing mid-life modernization of old frigates; all savings went into submarine building, the new Type 23 frigate and upgraded weapons systems. Far from reducing expenditure on the Royal Navy we increased it by £½ billion in the period from 1980 to 1983.

When it comes to punch-ups between politicians and the Royal Navy, nothing much changes over the centuries. Look at the rows between Admiral Lord Fisher and Winston Churchill, and those experienced by Denis Healey and Duncan Sandys, who lost his Chief of the Naval Staff. I nearly lost mine when Henry Leach briefed Jim Callaghan against the government. Margaret Thatcher insisted that I sack him, but I refused, saying it would cause more hassle than it was worth.

It is worth quoting what that constitutional grandee Walter Bagehot said in 1867:

> The Naval art and the military art are both in a state of transition; the last discovery of today is out of date, and superseded by an antagonistic discovery tomorrow. Any large accumulation of vessels or guns is sure to contain much that will be useless, unfitting, antediluvian, when it comes to be tried. There are two cries against the Admiralty which go on side by side: one says, 'We have not ships enough, no "relief" ships, no Navy, to tell the truth'; the other cry says, 'We have all the wrong ships, all the wrong guns and nothing but the wrong . . . '

During the course of a forty-year career in the Royal Navy, Admiral Lewin saw it shrink from the largest and arguably the most powerful navy in the world to its present reduced size. He saw the introduction of radar, the replacement of the battleship by the aircraft carrier and the introduction of nuclear-powered submarines like Polaris and Trident. He went through the Healey, Sandys and my defence reviews, including the cancellation of the Royal Navy's aircraft carrier programme by Denis Healey and their replacement by the so-called through deck carriers and the Sea Harrier, just recently phased out by today's new carrier programme. No service officer, not even Mountbatten when he was Chief of the Defence Staff, was so influential or important to the Royal Navy.

But one essential fact is always overlooked. In 1951 the naval budget, when we had a huge number of former wartime ships, amounted *at 1982 prices* to £2,564 million. By 1982 it had risen to £4,047 million including Trident, and the Navy's share of the total defence budget had risen from 25 to 29 per cent of the total. The reason, of course, was the increasing sophistication and cost of modern technology. Fewer ships and considerably more money. The notion that the Royal Navy was neglected in favour of the British Army and the RAF is nonsense. And Terry Lewin never complained to me about fewer ships, while his colleague Henry Leach, who was obsessed by numbers and not, as he should have been, with effective weapon systems on those ships, did. More on the Falklands later.

Before I revert to the Defence Review of 1982 and the subsequent Falklands War, I must mention how and why Terry Lewin went from a modest middle-class background to such eminence in life. He was born in Dover in 1920; his family had no connection with the Navy, and unlike the boys who joined him on an adventure visit to Newfoundland, he did not go to public school. Unusually, too, he did not go to the Royal Naval College at Dartmouth but joined as a Special Entry cadet at the last possible opportunity before the war at the age of eighteen, having failed to get into university. There was then a fair amount of snobbery about naval officers who had not been through Dartmouth.

When I first joined the Ministry of Defence, the Chief of the Naval Staff, Henry Leach, asked to see me about his career planning for the

Navy. He showed me a chart which identified the high-fliers with the executive class from Dartmouth. I showed interest and appreciation of this system but could not see how I could make a contribution. I told Henry Leach that several of my family had been to Dartmouth. He expressed surprise and pleasure that the new Defence Secretary had naval connections, but his appreciation of his new boss did not last long! This story illustrates the extraordinarily old-fashioned traditions of the Royal Navy. Terry Lewin abolished this class structure in the Navy, one of his more valuable contributions to the service. Can you believe it that Admiral Sir Lindsay Bryson was reputed to be the first naval engineer ever to be appointed to the Admiralty Board, and he was the best of the large bunch of admirals?

It is not possible here to list all the ships that Terry Lewin joined during his service, many of them famous. He started as a midshipman in HMS *Belfast*, which was destroyed by a magnetic mine and after recovery is now a museum moored along the Thames. He served on the battleship *Valiant* and survived Luftwaffe attacks off Norway. He took part in the destruction, on Churchill's orders, of the French fleet at Mers-el-Kebir. He joined several dangerous convoys in the Mediterranean to relieve Malta. After the war he captained the aircraft carrier *Hermes*, which later took part in the Falklands campaign. He was detailed as Executive Officer of the Royal Yacht *Britannia* . . . and tried to get out of it. The Queen said to him on arrival, 'You were the chap who didn't want to join my yacht.' He had wanted to be a sailor, not a cruise official.

But his greatest wartime achievement was his service on HMS *Ashanti*, a very lucky ship. He was on *Ashanti* when she was a member of a relief convoy to Malta and survived continual air attacks by the Luftwaffe. He was then involved in several Arctic convoys – PQ16, the disastrous PQ17 convoy where twenty-four of the thirty-nine merchant ships were lost, and then PQ18. The Admiralty gave much thought to the best way of getting this large convoy to Murmansk, in difficult conditions: there had to be sufficient daylight and fair weather, but this in turn allowed massive air, submarine and possibly surface attacks, mainly by German aircraft based in Norway. Six of the eight ships in one column were sunk by fifty-five Heinkel aircraft armed with torpedoes, but most of this convoy got through to the White Sea. It was then decided to return the empty convoys of PQ14, some ships of PQ16 and some survivors of PQ17, going far north of Iceland.

On the way back disaster struck and German U-boats scored several successes, as well as torpedoing HMS *Somali*, *Ashanti*'s sister ship. Captain Onslow decided to take *Somali* in tow 700 miles south to northern Iceland, but the towing cable parted. Lewin was foremost in trying to rescue the crew of *Somali*, but the story, recorded by Lewin, is rather tragic; only thirty of *Somali*'s crew were rescued alive, rigid with hypothermia, and forty others were lost, some beneath the keel of *Ashanti*. Sub Lieutenant Lewin was awarded the Distinguished Service Cross 'for services in *Ashanti* in taking convoys to and from Murmansk, through the dangers of ice and heavy seas and in the face of relentless attack by enemy U-boats, aircraft and surface forces'.

In war so much can be ghastly, but surely nothing has compared with the suffering of those who served on the Atlantic convoys to Russia. In my sketch of Inga (see Chapter 4) I also record the DSC won by my Cornish neighbour Lord St Levan, who served on minesweepers in the White Sea.

When Lewin became Chief of the Defence Staff, financial pressures dominated his time. There were three main concerns: the replacement of Britain's nuclear deterrent, for which there was limited financial provision; a review of Britain's defence structure in the light of heavy and conflicting demands for expenditure by the three services; and the higher organization of the Ministry of Defence.

Because it was agreed the deterrent was 'a political lever and not a military weapon system', there were widespread doubts about whether it should be afforded in the constrained budget available to the Ministry of Defence. But early on Lewin and Leach put their prestige behind the Trident weapon system and refused to accommodate the doubts about its need which had always been strong in the Army.

I had looked at the forward defence arrangements in what was known as the Ten Year Costings Programme, and I considered it completely unrealistic to imagine that the country, with all its economic problems, could possibly afford to extend the projected 3 per cent real growth for the whole ten years. I put it at five years. This caused immediate drama because the naval programme in particular had been organized on a ten-year projection. It led to what were known as 'cuts'; there were no cuts to the existing programme, but there was a need to reduce the forward order programme to a more realistic level in accordance with this country's real economic status.

I asked all three services to look at their programmes from the bottom up, setting out their priorities in order of need. I signalled that I could not accept the normal salami-slicing at the top. The Navy responded by saying their preference was to remove the Royal Yacht and HMS *Endurance*, knowing that these were politically the most sensitive for me to agree to! And so it went on. Then came the critical moment. Who was going to finance the cost of Trident? The Royal Navy was determined that it should be borne equally by all three services. As the Navy was responsible for Polaris, I decided that Trident must go on the Navy programme. Nothing caused more resentment and anger towards me than this decision.

Terry Lewin was well aware, as a former Chief of the Naval Staff, of the grief that these decisions were causing among the naval staff, but he did not intervene with me. Then, when it became necessary to reduce the forward naval programme by more than the Army and Air Force projections, the Navy's resentment grew. The reason was straightforward: I could not reduce the Air Force programme because its purchase of the Tornados was already contractually committed – and the Brussels Treaty had set out a minimum force structure on the Continent for the British Army of the Rhine.

Why do I recite all this? I don't want to fight old wars for the sake of it. I do so because it showed Terry Lewin at his finest. He was under intense pressure from the Navy, to whom he owed a lifetime of loyalty. I can best turn to the authorized biography of him by Admiral Hill:

> Inevitably the question, a critical one in the context of this biography, must be asked: did Terry Lewin at any time consider resignation, as the senior serving naval officer? More broadly, did he during the Nott Review fight hard enough for the service he so patently loved and had preserved, throughout his career, as a balanced autonomous force of worldwide reach?

The answer to the first of these questions is almost certainly No. None of Lewin's closest confidants have suggested that he seriously contemplated resignation.

The second question is more difficult to answer. It was posed countless times during research for this book, and many witnesses, from all the services and from political and civil life, either asked it themselves or readily discussed it – usually in the form 'Yes, why didn't he fight harder?'

One reason could have been that he was intellectually convinced of the rightness of the reasoning in Cmnd. 8288. That would have meant his full acceptance, strategically, of the overriding nature of the NATO commitment, the primacy of the Central Front, the inevitability of a short-war scenario, and the reduction of the Navy's role to an ad hoc sideshow; and at the grand tactical level, the early use of theatre nuclear weapons, the reduction in importance of transatlantic reinforcement, the abandonment of convoy, and entrusting anti-submarine warfare largely to a combination of air and submarine units that was untried in war.

Here I should say that when I travelled to Washington to talk about my Defence Review and the reduction in frigate numbers, Terry insisted that I join him at Norfolk, Virginia, the Headquarters of the Atlantic Command. There it became clear to me that escorted convoys of the Second World War type made no sense. It was probably inevitable, although a ghastly thought, that Soviet forces would reach the Channel ports within weeks unless we resorted to the use of battlefield nuclear weapons. The notion of a long war, sustained by convoy reinforcements from America, made no sense. The long war versus the short war in our planning caused much angst. In fact, with modern missiles, the surface fleet and our carriers would only have survived if they had joined the larger and better equipped US Navy in what we called the Iceland, Greenland, Norwegian gap.

Finally, I must quote again from Admiral Hill's authorized biography:

Lewin was Chief of the Defence Staff. It was his business to co-ordinate, within the limits of the organization, the defence interest as a whole. As Chairman of the Chiefs of Staff Committee, he had to take a strictly impartial position, reconciling, so far as he could, often radically different points of view without fear or favour. Any partisanship would be very quickly detected and his credibility with the other Chiefs would be fatally undermined. The fact that, in the circumstances of the Nott Review, the balance of opinion amongst his colleagues would almost always be two to one – the Army and Air Force against the Navy – would increase his difficulty in advocating any naval line.

I saw Terry Lewin several times towards the conclusion of the Defence Review. I do not recall him questioning the logic of Command 8288. He had a difficult time as Chairman of the Chiefs of Staff Committee because General Bramall and Air Chief Marshal Beetham were fiercely defending their own programmes, and, whatever his personal prejudices, he could not help out the aggrieved Admiral Leach. He was Chairman, not at that stage the government's chief adviser on defence with his own briefing staff.

He pleaded with me to defer the publication of the Defence Review, arguing that it needed more consultation among our allies. We visited NATO headquarters, where the principal concern remained the upholding of the Brussels Treaty. I told him that I had to get the White Paper on the Defence Review agreed by the Cabinet and published in Parliament before the summer parliamentary recess. He was concerned but understanding. His behaviour was impeccable.

Before the Falklands happened, he came to me with his proposal that the Chief of Defence Staff should be something more than the chairman of a committee representing the collective view of the Chiefs. It had not worked because it had become impossible to reconcile the opinions of the several Chiefs and Terry had no facilities with a central briefing staff of his own. In a speech to the House of Lords after his retirement he summarised the changes:

> I made proposals which were based on five principles. The first was that the Chief of Defence Staff should become the principal military adviser to the Secretary of State and to the Government

in his own right, and no longer as the chairman of a committee with collective responsibility . . . No longer would it become the fulcrum of collective responsibility . . . The Chiefs of Staff would remain the professional heads of their single services, responsible for their morale and efficiency. They would remain responsible for giving advice to the Secretary of State and to Ministers across the whole field of strategy, resource allocation and their own single service matters. They would retain their right of direct access to both the Secretary of State and the Prime Minister . . . The CDS had no staff of his own; he had only a staff which was responsible to the collective body. With these changes the central staff became accountable to the Chief of Defence Staff in his own right. At last he would have a staff of his own and could set it studies with terms of reference which he did not have to get agreed with all the Chiefs of Staff beforehand. The Chief of Defence Staff should become the Chairman of a senior appointments committee which would consist of the Chiefs of Staff. This committee would have responsibility for overseeing the promotion and appointments of all three- and four-staff officers.

I had been so frustrated by the inter-service rivalry and the inability of the Chiefs of Staff Committee to provide me with a recommendation for reducing the forward expenditure in Defence that I agreed to Lewin's proposals with enthusiasm. The Prime Minister endorsed this organizational reform – and it was published both inside and outside the Ministry of Defence. This change, proposed by Terry Lewin and disliked by the other Chiefs, was a necessary reform.

When the Falklands happened out of the blue, Admiral Lewin was in charge de jure and de facto. This proved to be critical to the management of the Falklands War.

Unexpected things happen in life and especially in politics. A war breaks out and the Chief of the Defence Staff is on the other side of the world, in New Zealand. Well, well! While I admired the confidence and leadership of Henry Leach, the Chief of the Navy, in telling Margaret Thatcher on Thursday evening, 1 April that he could set up a Task Force ready to go to sea by the following Tuesday, it was a moment when we badly needed Terry Lewin's presence in London. His quiet and considered approach to every issue, without too much Nelsonian dash, would have been invaluable in those first few days before the launch of the Task Force on the Tuesday.

Unlike Parliament, the Ministry of Defence remained calm in the crisis under the temporary chairmanship of Michael Beetham, the Chief of the Air Force. The only contingency plan available to me indicated grave doubts about our ability to recover the Falklands by force. I indicated as much to Margaret Thatcher alone with her in the evening. 'Whatever the risks, John,' she said, 'we must do it.' An urgent reassessment was undertaken of the size and strength of the Argentinian air force, and the viability of their naval forces; by the following week the conclusion was that, although the risks were huge, it should be attempted.

In retrospect, Henry Leach's determination to ready a Task Force within the next five days, coupled with Margaret Thatcher's courage, were two crucial factors that contributed to our later victory.

When Terry Lewin returned to London on 5 April a great deal of preparation had already been undertaken by the Central Staff. An outstanding admiral, John Fieldhouse, was given command and immediately set about the requisitioning of civilian cruisers and merchant shipping. His direct and personal link with Lewin, and through him to the commanders in the field, worked like clockwork. Fieldhouse became Chief of the Defence Staff a few years later.

In a crisis every outsider becomes an expert. Parliament did its best to cause trouble, not least because a substantial contingent of the Tory Party wanted the Prime Minister to fail. The Civil Service, champions at delay and forming committees, had been dealt a blow and never recovered. I had thought that we had far more admirals than ships, but the serving ones were disciplined – more than could be said for the very large number of retired admirals who all had a better solution to our problems.

The first disagreement was about the deployment of the press. In consultation with Terry Lewin and Henry Leach, I agreed that we should send a limited number, not least because satellite systems on the ships were needed for operations, not for journalists' despatches. There was a row, but No. 10 intervened to increase the numbers, so, to the distress of the Navy, we had no choice but to accept. In the end there were twenty-nine press embarked and six minders from the Ministry of Defence to provide security. It was the first time the press had been embarked in a maritime war – and generally they behaved well.

Terry understood two new principles of war. First, that there was no such thing as a military conflict – it was always politics, military and diplomatic – and he recognized that, in the future, the role of the media would be crucial, even if not entirely welcome to the soldiers and sailors in the front line.

Before Lewin's return from New Zealand, Margaret Thatcher formed a War Cabinet as the ultimate decision-making forum. It consisted of the Prime Minister, the Chief of the Defence Staff, the Deputy Prime Minister, Willie Whitelaw, the Foreign Secretary, Francis Pym, myself and Robert Armstrong, the Cabinet Secretary. We met daily at No. 10 and occasionally in the Ministry of Defence and at Chequers. It worked extremely well, and although there were endless differences between Pym and Thatcher, the atmosphere was civilized throughout.

There have been so many stories written about the war, including by me in my own memoir, that I will concentrate solely on Terry Lewin's contribution. He is, after all, the subject of this chapter.

He took it upon himself as the country's senior military adviser to coordinate and chair all the important meetings below the War Cabinet itself. He started his day with an intelligence briefing, which I also attended; he was then briefed by the military staff on the need for changes in the Rules of Engagement, with a substantial input from the Chiefs of Staff Committee; he was in touch continuously with Admiral Fieldhouse, the overall commander of the operation. He then had a tricky meeting every day with Permanent Secretaries and Foreign Office representatives before formulating his requests to the War Cabinet. He saw me, before the War Cabinet meetings, to ensure that he and I were in agreement and arguing the same case. It was a triumph of goodwill and persuasion before he brought his requests on the Rules of Engagement to the War Cabinet.

It was due to Terry Lewin's calm and intelligent persuasion that he and Thatcher forged such a warm relationship. By nature Margaret was aggressive and awkward, often rude to her colleagues, but the calm approach of Terry Lewin worked on the Prime Minister extremely effectively. Her courage and his calm advocacy were two crucial elements in the country's success.

I have considered many of Terry Lewin's achievements in his lifetime as a naval officer, but in closing I want to pull them all together. More than other naval officers he brought the Royal Navy into the modern era. The changes in equipment were dramatic. My own family – my uncle was a Dartmouth cadet and the last Chief of Staff of the Royal Indian Navy – introduced me to naval attitudes and customs. Retired admirals bark at you – and consider lesser mortals, particularly members of the Royal Air Force, to be members of a lower race. It must be the time spent at sea, difficult dockings and dealing with less than brilliant naval subordinates that gives them a sense of superiority over lesser land-based mortals. So among Terry's greater achievements was the creation of a General List, eliminating the class structure of former times. He wrote towards the end of this time, 'Equally dramatic was the Navy's social change' – it became more egalitarian, relaxed and family-conscious. He achieved this against much opposition from traditionalists, without losing the Navy's heritage. 'What I would like to be remembered for,' he said, 'is a real improvement of attitude and mutual respect between officers and ratings and the effect that this has had on the well-being and efficiency of the Navy.'

Another achievement was the creation of a much more joint-service approach to defence questions. The single services cling to their own identity, but now there are no single-service staff colleges; joint headquarters and operational command and control are common currency. Like all Defence Secretaries, I suffered from inter-service rivalry and distrust; it is diminished.

When Terry Lewin retired he undertook many important roles, not least the chairmanship of the Royal Navy College at Greenwich and the National Maritime Museum. I remember him talking to me about his naval hero, Captain Cook; he spent time in retirement researching this remarkable man.

But of the remarkable Terry Lewin let me conclude by quoting the final paragraph of Admiral Hill's biography. It seems to me to encapsulate perfectly the qualities of the man:

> His ready, real, immensely human sympathy seems to me to come close to the essence of this great man . . .
>
> The openness, the humour, the innate modesty and courtesy, combined with assured confidence to form a personality that was as lovable as it was commanding: but it all came from inside, it was totally genuine, a man of integrity and completeness, alive and whole.

Chapter Four

INGA

Berlin 1951

Possibly Inga was a tart, but I don't think so. I know nothing against her apart from a casual remark made by my Scottish batman. Tart or not, I have fond memories of her going back more than sixty years. Shortly after meeting her in 1951 I wrote a story about her which forms the basis of this chapter.

It must have been difficult in post-war Berlin for an attractive German girl. Berlin had been destroyed by the Russians only six years before; many German women had been raped; and cigarettes, soap and other requirements of a civilized life were in short supply. Berlin recovered quite quickly, however, and by the time I got there the British sector was beginning to get back to normal. The Russian sector was a disaster.

I was a second lieutenant in the Royal Scots; I was on probation, as it were, before taking a Regular Commission into the Gurkhas. We had a barracks opposite Spandau Prison and a company base at the top of the Kurfürstendamm. Berlin was huge fun for us soldiers. We had inherited German cavalry horses and took part in frequent horse trials; we went sailing in the Wannsee and spent many evenings around the recovering night clubs in return for half a bottle of gin. The Jocks, our Scottish soldiers, were mainly interested in drinking, beating up English soldiers when they found them – and, less so, in sleeping with German girls in exchange for a pack of five cigarettes.

I have placed Inga in this book in a place of honour between two Knights of the Garter and two OMs. Who knows whether, if any of us had been a young German girl in post-war Berlin, we would have behaved differently. I was eighteen and she was around the same age. Well, this is the story; here goes.

What really endeared the Royal Scots to me was the character of the Scottish soldiers. Colonel Melville, at my request, agreed that I should take my platoon on a six-week camp into the Grünewald, the fairly wild park (as it was then) on the banks of the Wannsee. There I subjected my young men to a rigorous training programme during the day, so much so that I was told at the end of it that they were the best trained platoon in the battalion.

Isolated as we were from the rest of the battalion, I got to know the Jocks extremely well. Apart from the NCOs, they were all National Servicemen from Glasgow (although the Royal Scots was an Edinburgh regiment). Most of these young men came from the Gorbals; physically small but wiry and tough, they had an excellent sense of humour but only three consuming interests in life – alcohol, fighting and women. Each evening, although I pretended ignorance of their leisure pursuits outside the camp, they used to get themselves completely plastered before seeking out English soldiers for a fight. If they failed to find their chosen opposition, they returned to the tented camp for a punch-up among themselves. By this time I was tucked up in my tent and I ignored their antics. However late and drunk the night before, they were always on parade in time, often bearing the scars of the previous night's affray. It may seem all rather shocking to today's climate of opinion, but these were the immediate post-war days and I admired the fighting qualities of my soldiers. I have always believed that Scottish solders are the best in attack and English soldiers for a dogged defence.

One particular episode at the start of my time camping in the Grünewald would linger long in my memory.

For three days I endeavoured to prevent our faithful band of female camp followers from hanging around the camp perimeter, but since they had every right to be there, there was nothing I could do to drive them away. The situation was made worse by the fact that they found me a source of constant amusement, and I had no doubt that they told dirty stories about me to the Jocks. Discipline was being undermined and the situation was undoubtedly getting out of hand.

I therefore circled the camp with barbed wire and absolutely forbade the men to bring any of these women inside the camp perimeter. I then turned a blind eye to their absence from the camp at night so long as they were present on parade, well turned out, by seven o'clock the next morning.

I may say that it was as much as I could do to maintain my temper. Although I was never so unfortunate as to actually witness any kind of disgusting act of love in progress, the bushes surrounding the camp often echoed with giggles and swear words in the German tongue.

Perhaps I should say here and now that the Jocks respected this concession to their animal impulses and kept their side of the agreement by working hard during the day and appearing slightly pale but well turned out on parade each morning. The sight of their women, however, continued to haunt me (although I must say quite a number of them were agreeably attractive).

About a week after our arrival at this spot I decided to take my jeep out one morning and make a reconnaissance of the edge of the lake in order to find a suitable place to practise a water-crossing exercise. It was a fine sunny day. The lake was perfectly calm and reflected the tree-lined hills quite beautifully. As I drove along the water's edge on this spring morning I felt contented, for my military training programme was going well, if yet somehow incomplete. Although at the time I was ignorant of what I lacked, you will realize that the stirrings of my manhood, buried under a public school training of many years, were beginning to make themselves felt. About three miles from the camp there was a small bay that suited my purpose admirably and I therefore left the jeep on the road and walked down to the water's edge.

As I did so, I passed a small boathouse and saw an old man of about sixty sitting beside it smoking a pipe. Wishing to find out exactly where I was, I approached him and said in the halting tones used quite inexplicably by the British when they wish to be understood by a foreigner, 'Do you speak English?'

'Nein,' he replied arrogantly, a proud man who had seen his nation beaten twice by the British but had never admitted defeat. Then, turning towards the boathouse, he shouted 'Inga!', and as a young German girl appeared in the doorway he pointed at me in an ignominious way with the stem of his pipe.

'Aha,' I said. 'Can you help me?'

'I will try,' she said in halting English, with a friendly smile.

Now you must realize that at the time this girl appeared to me to be nothing more than a direction finder in my efforts to find a suitable place for an exercise. I did not notice her as a woman, hardly as a human being. She might well have been described in an Army pamphlet as a 'local inhabitant of an area' who 'will often prove of considerable value in orientating your position'. Nevertheless, I will describe her now, although most of the details of her features and figure only slowly became evident to me in the two days that I knew her.

Although she must have been of medium height, the impression that remains with me is of a heavily built girl whose figure radiated a considerable voluptuousness. Her legs were strong and her calves thick and muscular. Nevertheless, she had a good waist and large soft feminine breasts that her dress contained with difficulty. Looking back on it, her face to an English taste would have appeared too full of expression and character. In fact, when I showed my sister a photograph of her face she described Inga as looking like a tart!

I do not believe that I have seen, ever again, such genuinely friendly eyes. They had a watery and greenish depth reminiscent of an alpine lake. Her mouth was large and the lipstick that she wore was a deep red that enhanced the roundness of her face.

But more than any other part of her body it was her hair that I quickly noticed, for it was a deep shining brown and it hung in an unkempt, rather stringy manner around her shoulders. This slightly dishevelled hair reflected boredom, incompleteness and adolescent disharmony with life.

It must, I suppose, have been the extreme sensuality of this girl coupled with her forthright and completely uninhibited approach that overcame my reserve and shyness. Very quickly we were discussing the beauty of the lake, the islands in its midst and the yachts that lay becalmed throughout its length.

Returning to the camp that night I felt a different man. The feeling of incompleteness that had worried me earlier in the day was gone. As I drove in the camp I passed a group of the men's women who giggled and whispered to one another in an attempt to embarrass me.

My arrogance was, however, by now complete, since, added to the adolescent pomposity engendered by my rank, I now also felt an inherent superiority over the Jocks and their whores. Before, although I despised these women and was revolted by their activities, I had had no girl of my own. Now I knew a clean, pleasant and wholly attractive German girl, who in her looks and conversation was suitable for a young officer.

That evening I ordered McDade, my batman, and three other men to inflate the rubber dinghy and to arrange for some sandwiches and a thermos of tea to be ready in the morning. At lunchtime the next day they carried it down to the water for me, and, having placed it on the beach, they returned and sat on the hill.

At two o'clock Inga came to meet me as I had arranged and together we pushed the boat into the lake and set off for a picnic. As I paddled away the four Jocks cheered, laughed and waved, and proud of my conquest I waved back laughingly, thinking how envious they must have been of my good fortune.

After paddling slowly across the lake for an hour I suggested to Inga that we land on a small island and eat the tea that I had brought. She gaily agreed. There for hours I toyed with her, uncertain and hesitant in my actions until she, realizing that she was in the hands of a completely inexperienced young man, took control and by suggestion and subtle innuendo indicated the parts of her body that gave her pleasure. However, it was not until darkness came that I could contain my embarrassment sufficiently to explore her buxom body with anything bordering on military precision, and even then it would have been difficult to tell who was the more active partner or love's leader.

As the lesson progressed through the gathering darkness, my confidence increased and, in the same way that an intangible bond grows up after two Englishmen have sat opposite each other in an otherwise empty railway carriage for four hours without speaking, conversation started, and we began to learn about each other and the background to our lives.

'My father and mother were killed by the Russians,' Inga told me, 'when they conquered Berlin, and something horrible happened to me. Now I live with my grandparents in Spandau, but they are very old.'

'Do you ever go out in the evening,' I asked, 'with any German boys?'

'There are very few German boys in Berlin,' said Inga.

'You speak such good English – I suppose you learned it at school?'

'Well, yes, a little, in fact all. What about you? You are an English officer and so nice – my grandfather would hate my going out with an English officer. I like the English though and especially the Scottish.'

'Do you know any of them?'

'Oh, only one or two . . .'

It must have been about midnight that we reached the edge of the lake and I walked up the path past the camp with Inga and on through the trees for a mile to the main road where I kissed her goodbye. And as I wandered back through the darkness I felt weighed down by sympathy for her life and the terrible tragedies of her youth. Yet at the same time the knowledge that she had confided in me, had given herself to me and had wept at the thought of my one day leaving her, engendered in me a kind of humility that until that day I had lacked.

But as I approached the camp my thoughts were rudely jerked back to the reality of my position and the responsibility that was mine with the men under my command. Sadly, I reflected how great could be the benefits that 'my Jocks' might derive from friendship with such a girl, instead of the incessant squalid acts of physical love in which they indulged with the half-human women of their acquaintance.

Wearily as I reached my tent I sank down upon my bed to find McDade faithfully awaiting my arrival with a mug of tea in his hand.

'Oh, well done, McDade,' I said. 'My goodness I'm thirsty. How did you guess how welcome this would be?'

McDade just grinned and said, 'I just knew, sir. Oh, how did you find her? A bit of all right, I bet.'

'Yes – jolly good,' I said quite startled. 'What do you mean?'

'Oh, only that we reckon Inga's the best bang in Berlin. Until tonight you were the only one in the platoon who hadn't bedded her. Goodnight, sir,' he said and disappeared.

My lesson was complete, but I doubt my batman's sense of humour!

*

I conclude with a story about a neighbour of mine in Cornwall, the late John St Levan, proprietor of St Michael's Mount. He was a great

Cornishman and was very kind to me. John was a delightful man and, like Admiral Lewin, had spent his early youth on the ghastly Russian convoys to Murmansk in the Arctic seas, when he, too, won the Distinguished Service Cross. John was serving in minesweepers and spent more than a year in the White Sea seeking out German mines. Because of the length of time spent there he was allowed ashore by the Russians to collect supplies. When I visited him at his home shortly before his death to talk about the convoys, he pulled a handkerchief from his top drawers – and said he had guarded it all his life as a prized memory of a Russian girl he met ashore. They only saw each other for a few days. As a result, he said, she was banished to Siberia and was never seen again. It is odd how the minor experiences of young men can remain in their memory all their lives.

Chapter Five

Lord Tebbit

Politician

Norman is one of nature's gentlemen, maybe not of the conventional English kind – he is no Sir Bufton Tufton – but a real charmer none the less. The media depict him as 'the Chingford skinhead', and Michael Foot's 1978 description of him as a 'semi-house-trained polecat' was amusing but could not be further from the truth. Parliamentary abuse of this kind is reserved for politicians who matter – and Norman mattered.

It is a long time since I served with Norman in the first Thatcher government – more than thirty-five years to be precise. The day after the Conservatives won the General Election in 1979, I had a call in Cornwall from Margaret Thatcher inviting me to become Trade Secretary – 'And would you mind,' she said, 'having Norman as one of your junior ministers?' I said that I would be delighted, but that one 'pilot' was enough when she then offered me Lord Trefgarne, another pilot. I didn't know Norman well at that stage, but we had cooperated in ousting Ted Heath in favour of Margaret Thatcher for the leadership of the Conservative Party. Norman became Under-Secretary in the Trade Department, responsible for aviation, shipping and tourism. He is kind enough to say that I did not interfere and left him to get on with it. In his memoir he is rather frank about my character. As readers of this book have to suffer the prejudices of the author, it is worth knowing what another politician said of me:

> I found John Nott to be a mercurial character with strong upbeat moods when he would tackle any issue with enormous energy, insights of lateral thinking, great style and determination. At other times, in his downswings, he was difficult to work with, listless, refusing to take decisions, a prey to defeatism claiming that, anyway, no decision would improve matters.

I accept the criticism that I sometimes refused to take decisions thrust on me by my activist junior ministers, namely Norman Tebbit, Cecil Parkinson, Sally Oppenheim and Reg Eyre; they were a good lot and very supportive of their boss. But I have to claim that *no* decision is often the right decision in politics. *No* decisions are always the most difficult to accomplish; colleagues, Parliament and especially the media are always clamouring for action. The twenty-four-hour media circus needs something new to say each day.

In the Terry Lewin chapter I explain my initial hesitancy about launching the Task Force to the Falklands. I think I was right to hesitate; the logistics initially seemed quite horrible. It soon became clear that we could do it, and I went from there.

Norman went on:

> The week after the election found John in splendidly upbeat style, gathering us all around the table in his office (to become mine only four years later) telling us that now was the time to take the critical and radical decisions. If we delayed, he said, we will be enmeshed in all the detailed arguments against doing anything, so let's get on. In no time at all we concluded that all controls over prices should go. This left the Price Commission without a role but we agreed that the question of its abolition would have to be further considered by the Cabinet. Although John faced some opposition from the old guard, who still hankered for incomes policy, I think none of us had any doubt about the outcome – and it soon went.
>
> John's appetite for radicalism suited me very well. There was a need for a Civil Aviation Bill in 1980 and I suggested we should use it to give authority to denationalise British Airways as soon as circumstances allowed. John took up the idea with great enthusiasm, although in the end he could obtain agreement only to the sale of a minority shareholding. His statement to the Commons on 20 July brought some predictable reactions of pleasure and fury from Opposition sides. We both enjoyed it hugely – we were the first ministers to nail our colours to the privatisation mast, just beating Keith Joseph's statement on

British Aerospace. Sadly the troubles of British Airways and the legal actions by Laker delayed the flotation until February 1987 but the process was under way.

Very few politicians stamp their authority on a new policy of lasting national importance; most go with the flow – and policies evolve but do not break the mould.

Norman, as Secretary of State for Employment, designed and fought through new policies for industrial relations that have had a positive and lasting impact on society, surviving Labour and Conservative governments. Since his radical changes to industrial relations the country has benefited from a remarkable period of stability. Norman went on to become Secretary of State for Industry and Party Chairman.

Norman left school at sixteen, working for a few years as a young number cruncher on the *Financial Times*, and then had the good fortune, like the rest of our generation, to be called up in 1949 for obligatory National Service. At that time 150,000 eighteen-year-olds were conscripted every year, mainly into the Army.

On Thursdays, all over England, decrepit steam trains pulled out of railway stations delivering their quota of raw recruits to Inverness, Darlington, Preston, Worcester, Brookwood and Aldershot. A mixture of Brummies, Mancunians, Cockneys, Jocks, Geordies, Borstal boys, illiterates and public school boys were thrown together in the barrack room in a sort of ordered chaos.

'I approached National Service with mixed feelings,' wrote Norman. Didn't we all? But it did Norman a world of good and set him off to a new career. He had the special fortune to be recruited into the RAF, as 2435575 Aircraftman 2nd Class Tebbit; to get into the RAF for National Service was something of a triumph. In 1949 the Cold War had begun and suddenly the RAF was facing a potential shortage of both serving and active reservist aircraftmen.

After the conventional humiliating start in a draughty barrack room presided over by a dictatorial corporal, Norman was chosen to become an officer cadet training to be a reserve pilot, as at that time pilots were in very short supply. He learned to fly various training aircraft, destroyed a Meteor aircraft as it overshot a runway, but survived with minor injuries. On leaving the RAF he became a junior navigator and then a pilot with BOAC, flying all over the world until he entered politics as the Conservative MP for Epping in 1970. It is a happy story.

Here I must diverge a little to comment on the long-forgotten world of National Service, which survived right up to 1960. It probably did more good than harm to most eighteen-year-olds; and we certainly all got to know each other regardless of class and education. Unfortunately it would be impossible to bring it back, but it would be wonderful for today's bored and spoilt youth to undergo the discipline, comradeship and ordered life of military service. A few like Norman and I benefited greatly by the experience; others found the tedium of military life a waste of time and an unwelcome interruption to their careers. Inevitably the periods of inactivity and leisure associated with military life led, for National Servicemen, to what would be described today as the 'laddish' pursuits of booze and women. In those days most young men were virgins on enlistment, but service in the Far East, the Middle East and Germany did not extend their innocence for very long. Did it do them any harm? I doubt it. To this day, I can identify my fellow countrymen who have spent a period of their life in military service from the vast majority who have never done so. Some senior politicians start their life today not in military service but in the Conservative Research Department. Oh dear! It shows.

There had been a long-held belief that damaging industrial action could best be curbed by wise trades union leaders in the TUC who had to be kept sweet, not only by 'beer and sandwiches' at No. 10 but by various concessions. It did not work. Nor, interestingly, at a later date, did Ted Heath's attempt at tripartite government during his Prices and Incomes Policy make any headway with the titans of the TUC.

I served on what was known as E Committee, consisting of around eight members of the Cabinet under Margaret Thatcher's chairmanship, where our policy towards the unions was endlessly discussed. Catastrophic industrial disputes were destroying the country and earned us the title of 'the sick man of Europe'. Jim Prior, for whom I felt considerable affection, not least because, unlike other so-called 'wets', he stood his ground against the Prime Minister, believed in a softly, softly approach towards the trades unions. His view was shared by others on the Committee, including Quintin Hailsham, then Lord Chancellor.

Several earlier attempts had been made to tackle Britain's endemic problems, not least by Barbara Castle in the Wilson government. It had been destroyed by Jim Callaghan and other trades unionists in the Labour Cabinet. Then Ted Heath came along and proposed an Industrial Relations Act which had the criminal law at the heart of its sanctions. Norman was against that Act and set out a more subtle approach via civil rather than criminal law. He believed that persuasion rather than confrontation was the most positive way to deal with fractious industrial disputes. At its heart Norman's plan involved the repeal of the 1906 Industrial Act. By that he opened up the funds of the trades unions to compensation for those damaged by any unlawful act by trades unions. Actions in tort could be brought against unions if the strikes fell into a new definition of industrial action.

Protection under the law was only granted when workers involved in action had agreed in a secret postal ballot. Non-union workers dismissed to enforce a closed shop were enabled to sue both their employers and the trades union concerned. Sympathy action by workers of other employers would open them to civil action for compensation. That provision ended the nonsense of Post Office workers refusing to handle mail from South Africa and the mass picketing of Grunwick premises at Rupert Murdoch's new printing works. Tom King completed Norman Tebbit's reforms when he was moved to the Department of Trade and Industry.

All of this is long ago, and is largely forgotten, except by the new Corbyn Labour Party, who wish to repeal the Conservative government's laws. In fact, Norman Tebbit's reforms, coupled with the economic policies introduced by Geoffrey Howe, saved the country, which had been steadily going downhill since the 'politics of decline' presided over by Harold Macmillan, the author of so many of Britain's problems. It is to the credit of Tony Blair's government that it made no attempt to repeal Norman's outstanding reforms.

Norman will perhaps be more remembered by his friends and former colleagues for the dedicated care that he has given to Margaret, his wife, terribly disabled in the Brighton bombing during the Conservative Party Conference in 1984. It destroyed her life and brought to a premature end a political career which might have been extended further had he not decided to give himself over to her care, in preference to his own career as a senior politician.

I met Norman and Margaret Tebbit on several occasions when they were both recovering from their long stay in Stoke Mandeville Hospital. We were fortunate to be guests together at the home of Georgie and Neville Bowman-Shaw at Toddington Manor in Bedfordshire. They were wonderful hosts, and on occasions Georgie had to handle the Tebbits, their children, several nurses, two Special Branch minders, a Private Secretary and other help. Norman gave constant attention to Margaret. Initially, Margaret could not feed herself and was completely helpless. We all share enormous sympathy for Margaret, but it is worth remembering that when Norman was rescued from the wreckage of the Brighton bomb he had lost his right hip and all his back teeth, fractured his shoulder blades and broken five ribs. He was in constant pain.

Margaret is much improved, although completely disabled. She can feed herself and manages to roam around in a mobile wheelchair; it is awful but not quite as awful as it was.

I want to tell the story of Norman's physical and mental courage, for, as well as almost daily visits to Margaret, who remained in hospital for another two years, he was also conducting his responsibilities as Secretary of State for Industry, initially from Stoke Mandeville Hospital for several months. But he suffered from gossip and rumours in the parliamentary lobbies that he would never return to full-time ministerial work. In his memoir Norman describes the courage that he needed when he returned to London to face a sceptical press and his parliamentary colleagues, not least the mental struggle when he returned to the despatch box in the House of Commons, a testing place at the best of times.

There are many happy stories of people's kindness to him and Margaret over this whole period. Edward Heath, a political opponent, together with John Smith, the Opposition spokesman, visited him in hospital, as did the Duke of Edinburgh, the Prime Minister and many parliamentary colleagues. One of the most generous colleagues was Jonathan Aitken – who offered to put together a much needed trust fund for the support of Margaret – and the Duke of Westminster, who offered them a house on his estate in London at very favourable terms.

The most touching story, however, is of Norman's Special Branch officers, who went far beyond their duty in assisting Margaret with her physical demands – and Callum, his Civil Service Private Secretary, who sat up late at night reading poetry to a sleepless Margaret.

Are there any lessons to be learned from the terrible experience of the Brighton bomb? It killed a delightful parliamentary colleague, Tony Berry; it killed John Wakeham's wife and nearly John himself, but he staged a remarkable recovery. It permanently disabled another parliamentary colleague, Walter Clegg. What so upsets me to this day is the gossip generated about Norman in the parliamentary lobbies. Since my time in politics I have believed that unattributable briefing in the House of Commons lobby is a pernicious tradition; it feeds all kinds of unpleasant and sometimes vicious gossip to the press who, naturally, lap it up and publish it. All briefings in the parliamentary lobbies should be 'on the record' so that the source of false stories can be traced back to its source. These unattributable briefings do so much to lead to a public mistrust of politicians, who are generally hard-working, decent people.

Another happy story is that it was at the Bowman-Shaws' house in Bedfordshire that Norman became a shooting man. It led to his excellent book *The Game Cook: Recipes Inspired by a Conversation in my Butcher's Shop*, published in 2009. Margaret Tebbit persuaded her husband to take up shooting to get him away from politics, for which she had never had much fondness! He did so, and goes on shooting expeditions to this day. According to Georgie Bowman-Shaw, Margaret regrets her advice because she does not see much of him at winter weekends.

The political dramas of the past do not generate much interest, least of all in politicians' memoirs. But Norman remembered his successes in his memoir, and so he should have done.

In his time at the Department of Trade and Industry he was responsible for helping to build a strong manufacturing industry by attracting Nissan in 1984 and other Japanese investors into this country.

There is a canard promoted by the French that Britain is mainly a service economy, when actually our manufacturing base is now larger than that of France. The 'Thatcher miracle' in which Norman played a major part attracted far larger overseas investment into Britain than into any other European country.

When Norman became Chairman of the Conservative Party he played the key role in winning the 1987 General Election for the Conservative Party, despite suffering from negative interference by Margaret Thatcher, when she panicked about the forthcoming result.

This was sad, and uncharacteristic of her, because in all the years that I served as one of her Ministers in Trade and Defence she never interfered with any of my decisions. I could not help noticing how under Major and Cameron the independence and authority of senior ministers was curtailed by undue and counter-productive control from No. 10. It is not the right way to run a government.

After Norman left the Commons for the Lords in 1982 he could not resist using his privileged access to the media to comment adversely on the regimes of Major and Cameron. It is well summarized in his book *Unfinished Business*, in which he pleads for a continuation of the Thatcher centre-right reforms. He gained the reputation with both governments of being something of 'an Essex bovver boy'. A good example was at the Conservative Party Conference in 1992 when he attacked the Maastricht Treaty to the delight of the audience. Gyles Brandreth's diary records:

> The talk of the town is Norman Tebbit's vulgar grand-standing barn-storming performance on Europe. He savaged Maastricht, poured scorn on monetary union, patronized the PM . . . and brought the conference (or a good part of it) to its feet roaring for more. He stood there, arms aloft, acknowledging the ovation, Norman the Conqueror.

It was worse when Norman was recorded as saying privately of John Major, 'He has the mulishness of a weak man.' He backed John Redwood against Major for the Conservative Party leadership in 1995. In 2005 he backed David Davis against David Cameron in the Conservative leadership election. Then, in January 2006, he accused the Conservative Party of abandoning the Party's true supporters on the right by suggesting that David Cameron was attempting to reposition the Party 'on the left of the middle ground'.

But where I wholeheartedly agree with him is that our political generation saw ourselves fighting back from the leftish 'politics of decline' represented by that ham actor Harold Macmillan. In particular, we agreed with Keith Joseph that a 'ratchet to the left' had driven politics since 1945, and we sought to abandon the meaningless 'middle ground' and replace it with a strong centre-right coalition, which was later demeaned by both Major and Cameron, both of the liberal left.

I don't know whether Norman Tebbit would ever have made a good Prime Minister, but he would certainly have been a front runner for the job had he not abandoned politics to care for his wife.

Chapter Six

Lord Rees

Scientist, Astronomer Royal

It is something of an impertinence on my part to have included Martin Rees in this book. I have met him on a number of occasions, particularly when he was Master of Trinity, my old college at Cambridge. But after several meetings, I cannot say that I know him well, perhaps because I am not a scientist. Like so many others, however, I have fallen victim to his charm and high intelligence. As he has progressed from a fellowship of King's to the less than arduous role of Astronomer Royal, to Master of Trinity, President of the Royal Society and recently to give the Reith Lectures, I have followed his books and ideas with great admiration. This sketch follows a talk that I had with him on a visit to Cambridge.

I recall the occasion when he addressed Trinity old boys at a luncheon held in the beautiful Nevile's Court overlooked by the Wren Library. I wrote down his opening remarks:

> We are meeting here in probably a more intellectually fruitful place than any other patch of ground in the whole world. For this is the college of Isaac Newton and philosophers like Francis Bacon.

More recently this single college has become the home of more Nobel Laureates than most other countries. Cambridge has 96 Nobel Laureates, 32 of whom were at Trinity. By birth France has 51, China 11 and Russia 17. It is remarkable that one college in one university should produce such scientific brilliance.

This unique academic distinction, coupled with its great wealth, estimated at £1.4 billion, more than double that of any other Oxbridge college, led the college, I think, to adopt a rather inward-looking approach to life. I remember that before Martin Rees became Master it was the only college in Cambridge which failed to entertain its alumni during the autumn gatherings of former pupils. I doubt that it was the arrogance of wealth, just an unwillingness, almost distaste, to trouble itself too much with the outside world. Martin Rees changed all that – and he told me that his greatest gift to his old college was to embrace the Trinity alumni in its work and achievements.

My next encounter was with the former Bursar, Dr Bradfield, who is rightly credited with greatly enhancing Trinity's wealth with the establishment of the Cambridge Science Park and the Port of Felixstowe. I was sitting beside him at luncheon when he asked me if I had read Martin Rees's book *Our Final Century: Will Civilisation Survive the Twenty-First Century?*

I did so – and I became an avid reader of Martin's books and articles.

In his Reith Lectures, which are beautifully summarized in his book *From Here to Infinity*, Martin Rees says that scientists are specialists, not polymaths. Like their forebears they probe nature and nature's laws by observation and experiment, and they should engage broadly with society and public affairs. How many scientists I wonder take such an expansive view? Martin's triumph is that, while popularizing the remarkable advances of science, he emphasizes that scientific knowledge must be applied ethically and to the benefit of mankind. Scientists, he says, must confront widely held anxieties that genetics, brain science and artificial intelligence may 'run away too fast'. I discuss some of these issues below.

Martin makes the thought-provoking point that the worldwide attempt to proscribe the import and use of illegal drugs is hopelessly failing. What better chance is there to control the dangerous excesses flowing from biotechnology? The deciphering of the human genome allows science to be misused to create new agents of mass destruction. The genetic blueprint of large numbers of viruses is stored in databases accessible to scientists on the internet.

The problem is that self-restraint seems unlikely for many scientists with a narrow focus on some area of pure science; it is even more difficult to locate some loner, some fanatic or social misfit with the mindset of those who now design computer viruses.

We need more scientists like Martin Rees with the ability to publicize these dangers.

Another fascinating insight in Martin's work has been the discussion which he generated about the particle accelerator at CERN. After spending £10 billion, what CERN is undertaking is frankly beyond the understanding of people who are not trained in physics. The scientists have at last discovered what they call the Higgs Boson, the 'God particle', but even the physicists do not wholly understand it. A few scientists (Joseph Lykken of the Fermi National Accelerator, for instance) say that the Large Hadron Collider could have produced a different vacuum which will then expand at the speed of light, destroying everything, obliterating the workings of reality.

I am told that CERN will help us to know more about the early moments of Creation in the Big Bang. But, although the theory of the Big Bang has been proved fairly conclusively, I still believe that Fred Hoyle was right – that the Universe has existed forever in a so-called 'steady state'. The scientists are in a frightful muddle over the Big Bang – were there many Big Bangs etc., etc.?

My greatest loss in life is that as a wartime student I was never required to study science, physics and biology, just Latin and Classical Greek; disgraceful really. I hugely lack a basic knowledge of the sciences. How can someone like me understand Quantum Theory? It is impossible.

It was while I was at school that the scientists were busy with the Manhattan Project at Los Alamos which led to the creation of the atomic bomb. Scientists land us with these inventions and then leave it to the politicians to solve the resultant dilemmas.

At our meeting in Trinity I could feel that Martin wanted to talk about nuclear weapons and the Trident project which took up much of my time in the Ministry of Defence. Unfortunately, nuclear weapons cannot be disinvented; nor perhaps can the advances of super-intelligence, more likely, I suspect, to destroy the human race than nuclear weapons. The advance to a society dominated by robots seems unstoppable.

When fixing up a date for my talk with Martin Rees I posed a provocative question to him: 'Would Darwin have thought that a move from human to mechanical beings was just part of the process of natural selection? Is it just another twist in the story of evolution – or will it lead to the sixth extinction?'

My lasting impression of our talk was of Martin's great humility and his fears for the future of humanity. There is something hugely appealing about his concern for the future of humankind. Interestingly, we did not discuss his foremost interest in the planets and the likelihood of alien life. It seems impossible for me, and possibly for him, to imagine that with billions of stars surrounded by billions of planets life in some form, probably in the form of machines, will not exist somewhere else. We are inexorably moving here in our own small world, in spite of limited resistance, to a world dominated by machines. Commercial pressures and competition among the major high-tech companies like Google, Amazon and Microsoft are in this race for winners.

Martin Rees has helped to establish a research group in Cambridge for the 'Study of Extreme Risks'. It has a full-time staff of clever young people and, only the day before I saw him, he had attended a gathering with a team from DeepMind, the branch of Google studying quantum computers and artificial intelligence under Google's Director of Engineering, George Kurzweil.

Kurzweil was recruited by Google to act as thought leader-in-chief in the company's pursuit of machine learning. He is a prophet for the concept of 'singularity'. It is predicated on the belief that machine intelligence will come to redeem the universe of its incalculable stupidity. Kurzweil paints a future in which technology becomes more powerful until such time as its accelerating evolution becomes the primary agent of our own evolution as a species – biological life is subsumed by technology.

Once singularity kicks in we shall no longer be helpless and primitive creatures; we shall gain power over our own fate, resulting in a world that is still human but transcends our biological roots. Machine intelligence will, by connecting computers into our brains and bodies, change the nature of the human experience. An observation first made in the 1950s was that the number of transistors that can fit on a single microchip doubles roughly every eighteen months. The process of Darwinian evolution is one of exponential growth based on the compounding of scientific discovery and knowledge.

What do Christians make of it? Perhaps they would claim that it is all forecast in the Book of Revelation. Indeed, religion seems to canter along behind scientific discovery, seeking compromise, and then rejecting it for its own survival.

Maybe 'transhumanism', as it is called, is far-fetched. But is it? Kurzweil predicts that machine intelligence will reach its pinnacle around 2045, when my youngest granddaughter will only be fifty years old. It is rather frightening, but so is DeepMind.

Martin Rees rather laughed at all this and said that he had no intention of being frozen in a Californian icebox so that he could witness the outcome of such scientific speculation.

He emailed me after our talk with what seemed to me to be a rather defensive message: 'I think my one-sentence reaction to AI is that I remain less concerned about Artificial Intelligence than about real stupidity and suspect that this will be the problem for a long time to come!' Personally, I suspect 'real stupidity' and commercial pressures will collide quite soon.

While on the subject of artificial intelligence, I asked him about what the Pentagon is up to with robots called 'Lethal Autonomous Weapons Systems' (LAWS). Stuart Russell, an AI professor at Berkeley, suggests that these weapons could be fully operative in just a few years: there is an important ethical decision here, whether to support or oppose this programme. It is one step only from a drone operated by a man thousands of miles from a target to a robot that is programmed to replace that man.

'Autonomous Weapons Systems' select and engage targets without human intervention: they become lethal when those targets include humans. It means that machines rather than humans can be placed in the front line – that must be appealing to the generals.

If an international treaty could be put in place, as happened with blinding laser weapons in 1995, we may go some way to controlling unacceptable advances in advance intelligence in the defence ministries of the USA, Britain and Israel.

One of the issues in *Our Final Century* which formed the basis of our talk was the forthcoming rise in the world population to nine billion; maybe it will stop there, because, outside Africa, the birth rate is declining below the replacement of 2.1 babies for each fertile couple.

No course of action will freeze today's climate. Change is underway and is certain to continue because of inertia in the global industrial economy and the climate system; we have already emitted into the atmosphere enough greenhouse gases to extend far into the future. Population growth and the energy consumption that accompanies it has become a dominant factor. Martin Rees's concern about climate change found its way into Pope Francis's Evangelical on this subject in which he played a major part.

We did not discuss the problems caused by the thawing of the Arctic permafrost. Thawing across the vast expanse of Canada, Alaska and Siberia is underway. This is happening via the Mackenzie River, which drains much of western Canada, and the Lena, Tamesi and Ob rivers that drain northern Asia and flow into the North East Passage across Siberia; eventually all the fresh water will dilute the Arctic seawater and make it less likely to sink, impacting on the circulation of the tropical seawater from the Caribbean – that is 'our' Gulf Stream. Huge quantities of methane are being released from the melting permafrost; methane is possibly the most dangerous greenhouse gas of all. We have to find a way to make invention and adaptation possible, which means that we must foster the creation of wealth, which inevitably involves fossil fuels.

Martin and I did not fall out over the issue of fossil fuels. Martin is an avid supporter of reducing their use, but I protested that without oil-based fertilisers and agrichemicals the Green revolution which feeds the world's population today would hardly have been possible. He believes that with the benefit of new technology in agriculture and different techniques we should be able to feed nine billion people; I hope he is right. But it means a move from meat-eating to vegetarianism, against all current trends; much greater research about how warming weather can impact favourably on seed germination; how we develop crops more suited to more or less water availability and fewer fertilisers. Monsanto are making a greater contribution to combating climate change than all the morbid climate forecasters put together.

I do not think that, in their race for alternative energy, the climate scientists quite appreciate that if world wealth is sharply reduced, then the developed world will have less ability to assist the poorer nations to transfer to less polluting energy consumption. If the United Nations' own estimates are to be believed, world GDP should see a multiple increase in the next hundred years, not least through the application of modern technology. It is impossible to conceive of the world being able to finance a total replacement of fossil fuels by nuclear energy, currently the only economic alternative to gas and coal.

The Chinese have made admirable moves to reduce CO_2 in the atmosphere, but the Chinese only have an annual GDP per capita of $6,894, against $39,105 for the Euro area and $52,194 for the United States. It is hardly surprising that the Chinese have doubled the number of coal-fired stations in the last ten years. But they are onside, unlike the President of the United States, the greatest polluter of them all. I'm afraid there is an awful truth in the expression 'warmer and richer – cooler and poorer'.

As I was leaving Martin's rooms after our conversation, he stopped me on the stairs and asked me if our nuclear deterrent was genuinely independent. It was a cry of concern. I said that many people working in the software field believed that the Americans tampered with the missiles when they were under service in the United States. 'Surely,' he said, 'the Americans must wish to control our ability to release a weapon of mass destruction? Is the Trident weapon system genuinely independent?' This issue is obviously a matter of constant attention when we recover the system after service in America. In fact, the Americans have always felt that deterrence is enhanced by a second independent decision-making process. Why should the Americans wish to change their long-held policy? It was not an answer that Martin wanted; he wanted control and not dispersed decision-making.

My lasting impression of this remarkable man is that all his beliefs and actions stem from the heart. He has written and spoken widely of the wonders of modern science – of how it has accelerated exponentially even in the past decade. He has travelled much more widely than in his own field of astronomy, into biotechnology, population growth, climate change, artificial intelligence and the origins of our biosphere. He has opinions on all of them – and is not cautious about expressing his concerns about our progress into a dangerous new world. I wish we had more scientists like him, but I fear that all but a few have their heads buried in their laboratories as they seek inspiration and answers in their own narrow field. I doubt if he can be very popular among his peers, although all of them admire him for his candour and intelligence.

We had an exchange of emails before and after our talk, but his final email to me was to say how much he regretted that we did not cover the subject of the Conservative Party in our talk. Oh dear, how could he be interested in the Conservative Party?! He described himself as Old Labour – and a member of that party. I said that as a Conservative and Brexiteer – and that shocked him – I felt more comfortable representing the people of Sunderland than voters in Cambridge, Canterbury and Kensington! He laughed. Yes, the Brexit voters in Sunderland had a bad time in life, he said.

I have met many interesting people in my long life, but this man comes out top.

Chapter Seven

Sir Robin Day

Broadcaster

I set out with the intention of praising all my chosen victims in this book, but I have had some difficulty with Robin Day. I enjoyed his loud, cheerful personality, which I could hardly avoid as a Cabinet Minister in the 1980s, his high time as a celebrity. I must have appeared several times before the Grand Inquisitor, his own description of his role. My wife and I had him to dinner at our home on a number of occasions, so it was more than a purely professional relationship. Robin was good company, anxious to dominate the conversation and show off his fertile mind. I am not sure that he ever moved on from his triumphs as President of the Union at Oxford; I fear that it is a failing of many Presidents of the Oxbridge Unions, of which I myself am one! His spiritual home was the luncheon table in the Garrick Club among actors, barristers and other fellow performers.

My other difficulty is that in my Introduction I stated that what united all the personalities in this book was their evident integrity. I have to look again at that claim for I am not sure that it is an entirely accurate description of Robin Day. I think he was always prepared to cut corners to win in conversation, whether in private or in public on television. The desire to win in every encounter, while admirable in a grand inquisitor, could be an unattractive trait to the dispassionate observer. And he established a pattern which, in my opinion, we still suffer from today. The interviewer should tease out information and opinions; he or she does not need to win.

I felt that I should include Robin Day in this book partly because his name would arouse curiosity, but also because I was personally involved in what was later considered to be one of his most famous interrogations. In *Grand Inquisitor* he was rightly proud of his interviews with the Pope,

Gorbachev, Thatcher, Reagan and a host of other leaders, but no mention was made of a much lesser person – me. This provoked a very strong reaction, so his publisher insisted that our interview should be included in all subsequent editions. At the end of the interview with me, when he was losing the debate, he pulled out the phrase 'Here today, gone tomorrow' to describe me as a politician who had just announced his decision to leave Parliament. If it was a low blow, I did not mind a bit, and I saw him personally at home thereafter. When he had sadly lost his earlier ebullience to poor health, I chose the phrase as the title of my memoir. The opening paragraph read:

> Most politicians have five minutes of fame before they disappear for ever. My descent into obscurity was, however, suspended for several years as a result of walking out of a rather silly interview with Robin Day. It seemed then, and still seems now, to have been an incident of utter triviality. But the BBC, as an entertainment medium, thrives on triviality, and it therefore thought fit over a period of almost twenty years to replay the conclusion of the interview repeatedly.

It would be tedious to set out the full text of the interview, some thirty years after the event, but it began as follows:

> Sir Robin Day: Mr Nott, is it not remarkable that whereas in the conference agenda there is resolution after resolution calling on you to re-think, re-assess, re-examine, reverse, re-appraise your defence policies in the light of the Falklands conflict, none of this came out? Do not many of the resolutions reflect the criticism publicly made by Admiral Sir Henry Leach, the First Sea Lord, saying that we've got to retain the three Invincible class anti-submarine carriers, we've got to improve the effectiveness of weapons on destroyers and frigates, and retain, you know, more of them?
>
> Rt Hon. John Nott MP: You'd hardly expect the First Sea Lord to say anything else, would you?

RD: One of the criticisms (again reflected in the conference resolutions) by Sir Henry Leach is that the Navy is saddled with the whole of the Trident missile costs.

JN: But as you say, it didn't come up in the debate.

RD: No, well it ought to have done, oughtn't it?

JN: No, I don't think so. It's for the speakers themselves to decide what they wish to say, not what the media want them to say.

RD: On the merits of the point, for the benefit of many Conservatives and others, who are worried that the Navy may be saddled with too much of the Trident missile costs and will, therefore, be run down more than it should, what's the answer to that?

JN: Well, the Navy – the real sum of money we're spending on the Navy today is very much greater than when we came into power. On the conventional Navy, without nuclear weapons, it's about half a billion pounds more than when we came to office, and the Navy's share of the total defence budget will remain at around about a quarter of the total defence budget, in our forward plans.

This needled him; his attempt to set the agenda of our debate had been blocked, by a politician.

Robin's finest hour would come, but sadly he would never know it because it arose in a number of his obituaries; the best being a sycophantic piece by the excellent Dick Taverne, an MP and television interviewer himself – a member of the club:

He was the most outstanding television journalist of his generation. He transformed the television interviews, changed the relationship between politicians and television, and strove to assert balance and rationality in the medium's treatment of current affairs . . . In the pre-Day era, television interviewers were almost always respectful, generally dull and stiff, often insipid. Day asked the direct question pointed like a dagger at the jugular.

Such was his interview with ex-President Truman: 'Mr President, do you regret having authorized the dropping of the atomic bomb?'

This is a good example of the interview technique very much established as Robin's own style. If you think about it, it indicates the superficial nature of television questioning. How could Truman positively answer such a question without going deeply into the state of the war with Japan, the national characteristics of the Japanese and the option of destroying Japan by other means? Whatever response Truman gave would appear insipid. It showed that television reduced complicated issues to the soundbite and the quip, and Robin was good at it. Indeed, he can now be seen as the instigator and creator of soundbite politics. In a contest between a politician and an interviewer, the latter would nearly always win. But why do interviews need to be a contest? Robin Day moved politics from Parliament on to the television screen, leading to the soundbite television that we still suffer from today.

A. N. Wilson in the *Daily Telegraph* gave a more useful analysis of Robin Day's contribution to political debate. Day was successful, he said, in making the television studio, and not Parliament, the natural forum for political debate. Hugh Gaitskell, Harold Wilson and Ted Heath showed no unwillingness to be grilled by Sir Robin:

> He offered them a taste of the drug which was already sending him half mad with vanity, namely television fame.
>
> Yes, Sir Robin probably did contribute to the decline in importance of the parliamentary debate. That might well have happened in any case. The real sin which he carried around like an appalling dead albatross around his neck, was that he had helped to make the broadcasting medium into a so-called political forum. His own sublimely entertaining *Question Time* was so much more interesting than Question Time in the Commons that all politicians wanted to be on it. More and more political programmes had to be invented to accommodate them.

In the years when he was King of the Interviewers, it must have seemed to Day, as it seemed to us fans, that he was a far more considerable a figure than the mere politicians whom he cross-examined with that mixture of hectoring courtesy and devastating irony. In latter years, he discovered, sadly, that television fame is just as ephemeral as political fame, and that there were many young people who were not even aware of his existence. If he got his reward of a knighthood for the dubious distinction of raising the profile of also-ran politicians, he was intelligent enough to know that even the greatest television personalities, like politicians are, in his famous phrase, 'here today and gone tomorrow'.

That is rather a rough comment on the undoubted talent and skill of Robin Day. But I wondered, as I wrote, whether I was not being a little unfair to a major figure of his day, so I got together with one of his greatest personal friends to discuss his background.

Robin trained as a barrister after leaving Oxford and he had a lawyer's ability to get to the point of an issue very quickly. He had a quick mind and an ability to identify the weakness of his victim. At his daily lunches at the Garrick he surrounded himself with other barristers, journalists, playwrights, actors – all performers. Like so many actors he had a large ego and extreme insecurity. He did not lead a healthy life: he always had a cigarette or a cigar in his hand. This lifestyle began to tell and he died too young.

At the BBC, the directors and producers did not find him an easy colleague, and he did not treat the people behind him with sufficient courtesy. After all, he was a Star, and he knew it, so the BBC moved him on to handle *Question Time*, which he made a personal triumph. He had the ability to draw out the speakers and the audience – to bring in the vox populi. It was a great success for the BBC, and totally unexpected.

I think Robin never quite forgave himself for his failure to become a politician. He stood as a Liberal candidate for Parliament but did not make it. Throughout his career, however, he understood politics and always showed respect for politicians – even when he was trying to show them up in interview. That contrasts quite sharply with the Paxmans and Dimblebys of today – and some of the members of the morning *Today* programme – who exude a contempt for politicians and the necessary compromises required by the democratic process.

I suppose, in conclusion, that I have several problems in giving an unbiased picture of this substantial BBC figure. The first is that I find the smugness of the BBC and many of its performers quite hard to take. The organization is hopelessly failing and is unable to compete successfully with Sky, Al Jazeera and other independent stations. It needs root and branch reform. I do not accuse it of bias in reporting; it tries quite hard to be fair to every side and that must be quite difficult when the only newspaper acceptable to the staff and managers of the BBC is the *Guardian*, also failing! The only solution to the deep-seated problems of the BBC is to abolish the licence fee and throw the organization into the real world to compete – that would rid it of its smugness and sense of superiority.

Secondly, I think it is regrettable that Robin Day's great success in bringing politics into the television studio has dumbed down the political process. The best performers are the people who have mastered the soundbite. Time on the television screen is constrained. There is real concern that the listening public suffer from a very short concentration span – and there is no great gain in tackling political issues in any depth.

Robin, without intending it, created soundbite politics. Fortunately, the world moves on, and 'traditional' journalism is being superseded by social media. What remains both exciting and astonishing is the ability of the British electorate to come to conclusions independently of the media. That seventeen million people rejected the media and voted to leave the EU was a triumph of British democracy. It is astonishing how the British electorate always seem to get the right result.

Chapter Eight

Humbahadur Thapa

Gurkha soldier

Humbahadur was a Gurkha soldier. I met him first in the Malayan jungle in 1954; he was carrying a heavy Army wireless set No. 19 weighing 80lb or so. We plodded day by day through the jungle seeking to kill 'the bandits', as we called them, Communist terrorists who were trying to free Malaya from colonial Britain. Humbahadur was also carrying his personal haversack for a five-day operation which must have added to a total load of 120lb, not an unusual burden for a young Gurkha from the high hills of western Nepal.

It was touch and go whether we made wireless contact with Headquarters. Humbahadur, the signaller of our platoon, would throw an aerial over the nearest tree and, depending on our position in the steep hills of central Malaya, communication would be spasmodically successful, always in Morse code. We explained our position and the ground we had covered in the day; and received back any relevant information such as the position of a bandit camp which might have been spotted by an Auster aircraft flying over the jungle canopy.

After five days or so we often asked for an airdrop of extra food and supplies. Jungle boots and clothing did not last long. The Gurkhas carried sufficient food for several days, rice and *dahl* with maybe some dried fish. We ate breakfast before leaving the overnight camp and had the main meal when we ceased patrolling before dark. These airdrops were an interesting affair, requiring us to mark out a jungle clearing, and they were generally successful although several parachutes got caught in the trees.

Extraordinarily, I received an English food allowance throughout my time in Malaya although I much preferred to eat Gurkha food; the allowance mounted up in value and helped to pay my way through Cambridge!

When a smaller Army wireless set was introduced in 1953 I was withdrawn from the jungle and asked to form a new signal platoon to teach the riflemen of the battalion how to use it. Humbahadur was one of a team of fifteen men sent by their Company Commanders to learn the ropes from me, an ignorant second lieutenant with no training at all. I got to know Humbahadur rather well; for several months he was the best of a young enthusiastic team. We lived together in the same camp.

Long after I left the Army Humbahadur became the Gurkha Major QGO (the senior Gurkha officer) of the 1st Battalion, 2nd Gurkha Rifles and retired as an honorary lieutenant of the British Army in 1980. More of him later.

I talked to Humbahadur's son, Sergeant Bhakta Thapa, retired from the 6th Gurkha Rifles, to learn more about the family background. He now lives in England thanks partly to Joanna Lumley. Here his young family has the benefit of schooling and medicine, both virtually non-existent in Nepal during Humbahadur's youth.

Places like Aldershot are now home to many Gurkha families. Personally, like most former British officers, I think that Joanna Lumley, the attractive actress daughter of a former Gurkha officer, has actually done little service for these families, who otherwise would be living relatively well on former Gurkha pensions in the rather glorious foothills of the Himalayas. However, this is a complicated and emotive subject which does not fit here, and it is the choice of the Gurkha families themselves to come to Britain.

I came to join the 2nd Gurkha Rifles as a regular soldier in a rather unusual set of circumstances. I was a National Service officer in Aldershot when I decided, partly due to family history, that I wanted to join the Gurkhas. My old Victorian aunt, who retired to bed at the age of sixty and never got up again, had a close evangelical friend called John Crocker; he happened to be the Adjutant General of the British Army. When I told him of my ambition, he said that I would need to take a Regular Commission and spend a year on probation with the Royal Scots, an affiliated regiment of the Gurkha Rifles. I did so (see the chapter on Inga).

Later I reported for interview to General Sir Francis Tuker, the Colonel of the 2nd Gurkha Rifles. Tuker, one of Montgomery's favourite

Miloska, 1968.

Above: Lord Rees of Ludlow OM, Astronomer Royal, Former Master of Trinity, President of the Royal Society.

Left: Margaret Thatcher.

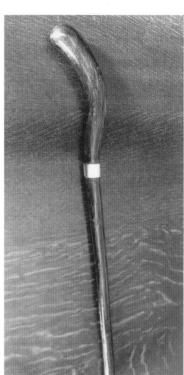

Above left: My Scout car in Malaya with (probably) Rifleman Humbahadur Thapa. (Photo taken by Colonel Jimmy Roberts MC, the founder of Mountain Travel in Nepal).

Above right: The silver band reads: 'Major (QGO) H. B. Thapa'. A gift to the author in Hong Kong.

Right: 2nd Lieutenant, 1st Battalion the Royal Scots; escort for the battalion train to Berlin, 1951.

Above: Douglas Shilcock on the unannounced visit to King's Mead of King George V and Queen Mary.

Left: Douglas Shilcock.

Captain (later Admiral) Middleton and the author on HMS *Hermes* three days before she sailed for the Falklands. *Private Eye*'s cover captioned the photo as follows: Middleton: 'What are the orders, sir?' Nott: 'We launch a surprise attack in three weeks time.'

Above: 2nd Gurkhas' Dinner. Defence Secretary (formerly Lieutenant) Nott, Prince Charles, Colonel-in-Chief, and General Bramall, Colonel of the 2nd Gurkhas.

Below left: David Omand on Ascension Island at the outset of the Falklands Campaign.

Below right: Michael Charleston.

Above: Billy Collins.

Below: Admiral Fieldhouse, Commander of the Falklands Task Force, and the author during the campaign.

Miloska in the daffodil fields on Trewinnard Farm.

Divisional Commanders, had been General Commanding the 4th Indian Division throughout the Desert War from Alamein and later into Italy, where the battalion lost a large number of its soldiers in a single attack on Monte Cassino.

I know the hills of western Nepal reasonably well after several visits, but I needed to understand where Gurkhas like Humbahadur came from. Sergeant Bhakta Thapa told me about the mountain village where his father was born. It is called Dhobadi and used to lie about two days' walk south from Pokhara. There is now a road.

To understand the history of western Nepal, I read many books, but none was more interesting and better informed than General Tuker's, published in 1957, *Gorka: The Story of the Gurkhas of Nepal*.

The Gurkha soldiers, who were recruited by the East India Company into the Indian Army from 1815 and are now recruited by the British Army into the Royal Gurkha Rifles, are mostly of mixed Mongolian descent. They retain a sympathy for Buddhism, which they practised before the arrival in Nepal of Rajput refugees fleeing the Turko-Muslim conquests of India in the thirteenth century. The local tribes were known as Gurungs and Magars, the former being gentlemen yeoman farmers who grazed their animals in the high pastures in the summer before returning to their modest homes for the cold winter months. The Gurungs, in particular, arrived in early history over the mountainous Himalayan passes seeking food, peace and land from turbulent times in Mongolia and Tibet. The Magars, like Humbahadur Thapa, tended to settle in the lower hills on land south and west of Pokhara, now the second most populous city of Nepal.

I do not think that a better description of the Gurkha can be found that given by one Colonel Vansittart in 1894:

> The Magars and Gurungs are of Tartar race; they live in Nepal, and follow agricultural pursuits, they are square built, sturdy men with fine muscular development and large chest and limbs, low in stature and with little or no hair on face or body, and with fair complexions. They are a merry-hearted race, eat animal food and in Nepal drink a kind of beer made from rice, and a kind of spirit called 'raksi'. They will drink any English wine, spirit

or beer. They are intensely fond of soldiering. They are very hardy, and extremely simple-minded. They are kind-hearted and generous and, as recruits, absolutely truthful. They are very proud and sensitive and they deeply feel abuse and undeserved censure. They are very obstinate very independent and very vain. They are intensely loyal to each other and their officers in time of trouble or danger.

It is extraordinary that I, tall and skinny with poor muscular development, can ever have commanded men like this, but they seemed to have respected me, as the story will tell!

The Rajput refugees from the Turko-Muslim invasions of India brought Brahman Hindu customs and the caste system with them into Nepal; there was a difficult fusion of Hindu practices into the animist beliefs which the local tribes shared with Lamaic Buddhism. I recall that although each Gurkha regiment had a Brahmin priest attached to it, the mumbo-jumbo of Hinduism was met with limited respect by the Gurkha soldiers, who used to joke about it among themselves.

However, the structure of the caste system placed the warring tribes of Nepal like the Gurungs and Magars of western Nepal into the Kshatriyas rank, below the Brahmins but above the merchant class of the common man and the menial castes. After the conquest of Nepal by a race of part-Rajput warriors from the town of 'Gorka' in Eastern Nepal, the Magars and the Gurungs were confirmed as a tribe of warriors who preferred soldiering and the spoils of war to the tedium of weaving blankets, tilling the fields and minding their flocks! Hence the clash between these warrior tribes and the attempt by the East India Company to secure and pacify its northern borders.

Back, then, to Humbahadur.

He became the Gurkha Major of my friend General Peter Duffell when he commanded the first battalion of the regiment in 1977. Humbahadur was a handsome man, and I include here a photograph of him with Margaret Thatcher when she visited the battalion. Humbahadur, like other riflemen, was keen on dancing at ceremonies, when they divided themselves into men and women. One of the burdens that I suffered with the Royal Scots was a similar habit when the young officers at mess nights divided themselves into men and women to dance Scottish reels. Awful for an Englishman!

The Gurkha Major of a battalion is a most important man, always greatly respected by the British officers and the Gurkha riflemen. I seldom saw Humbahadur's predecessor, Gurkha Major Bharti Gurung MC, who ruled over the regiment when I undertook my service in the early 1950s. He was always the confidant, adviser and friend of the battalion Colonel – and presided over the Gurkha officers' mess, which consisted of the other Gurkha officers who generally served as platoon commanders. In a way they were similar in importance to the senior non-commissioned officers who are the key to the success of the British Army.

Although the soldiers spoke several dialects in the hills of Nepal, when they joined the British Army tribal languages were discouraged. Everyone had to speak Gurkhali, a Sanskrit language. In my day the English language was largely unknown and joining British officers were sent off to learn Gurkhali so that they could communicate with their men. I received a language allowance throughout my time in the Army. Nowadays, when the Gurkha battalions are much more integrated into the British Army, English is essential and forms a major part of the education of the young recruits. I was reminded by Peter Duffell that, as a young officer in a Scottish regiment, I was regarded as a toff by my Glaswegian-speaking Jocks because I spoke a different dialect from them.

In the mid-1970s Captain Humbahadur was appointed a Queen's Gurkha Orderly Officer. Two senior Gurkha officers are appointed annually to this post and are required to attend the Queen at investitures and other official functions.

The history of the role is interesting. It seems to have stemmed from Queen Victoria's affection for and loyalty to her *munshi*, Abdul Karim. She made him her Indian clerk and secretary, to the fury of her courtiers who regarded him as an ambitious upstart. He certainly invented all sorts of stories about his background in India which were investigated by her jealous entourage. Queen Victoria had lost her faithful Scottish ghillie John Brown – and the *munshi* seems to have replaced him in her affections!

When Edward VII ascended the throne 1901 he commanded that his Indian servants, who included two Gurkhas together with Rajputs, Mahrattas, Pathans and Sikhs, should be called 'King's Indian Orderly

Officers'. They took their turn at the King's death and lying-in-state, stationed around the catafalque with officers of the Household Cavalry and the Foot Guards. King Edward VII had been the Colonel in Chief of the 2nd Gurkhas and was followed by Prince Charles in recent times.

I think that Humbahadur had visited England before at the barracks in Church Crookham, Hampshire, but contemporary British society was something of a shock to him. He was what we described as a 'Sidha Gurkha' – a very straight gentleman. He found the scene a little difficult to handle, for he was not a modern man. The young Gurkhas in the barracks were subject to all kinds of temptations with the local girls and in gambling, a favourite vice in Nepal. It was a clash of cultures.

Humbahadur, whom I knew first when he was a rifleman signaller, I met again as Gurkha Major of the battalion in Hong Kong when I visited it in 1980 as Trade Secretary. He was charming and welcoming, presenting me with his personal cane bearing his name on a silver band. It remains a valued possession of mine.

The final trigger for his inclusion in this little book of memories is when I visited Pokhara in Nepal as Defence Secretary in 1982 just before the Falklands War. Humbahadur had retired back to the hills but heard that I was in the country. Unbeknown to me he rallied a team of ten retired officer signallers whom I had trained in 1953 and they walked several days from their homes in the hills to give me dinner. I shall never forget the way they remembered me from thirty years before. It was an emotional occasion.

I can best conclude with a dinner given by the Gurkha Welfare Trust on 15 November 2017 to celebrate its vital work for retired Gurkha soldiers, especially in Nepal, a very poor country. Prince Harry, the principal guest at the dinner and who had served with the Gurkhas in Afghanistan said:

> The men of the Royal Gurkha Rifles are some of the most caring, humble and courageous soldiers I have ever had the privilege to meet; they are an inspiration to anyone fortunate enough to meet them. I am honoured to call them my friends.

Donations to the Gurkha Welfare Trust can be made via its website: www.gwt.org.uk

Chapter Nine

Michael Charleston

Journalist and fisherman

My first thought was to include Michael in this book as an honest
journalist, something of an oxymoron. As a former politician
I have known many journalists, and some have even been my
friends. But press journalism is in sharp decline; the mad twenty-four-
hour information circus has all but destroyed the traditional newspaper.
It has been outpaced by modern developments, not least social media and
the smartphone. The young don't read newspapers.

In Michael's day (he's now in his late eighties) the *Daily Express*,
which he joined in 1956 after six years on the *Western Morning News*, had
a circulation of over four million and competed with the *Daily Mirror*
as the largest daily paper in the Western world. Today the *Sun* has a
circulation of 1.6 million, the *Daily Mail* 1.5 million and *The Times* a
mere 450,000.

When Michael started as a journalist, the BBC was as complacent as
it is today; nowadays, it is left trailing by Sky News and Al Jazeera for
quality reporting. Its guaranteed income from the licence fee does it no
good at all. When Michael was young the BBC prepared a radio news
bulletin in the morning – and would have been surprised to make many
changes as the day continued.

The *Express* had a quite different approach. Lord Beaverbrook, the
very active owner, had a huge banner placed to span the big newsroom
of the *Daily Express*. It read: 'Make it fast, make it accurate.' The paper
changed and updated its editions all through the night. Beaverbrook paid
the top wages in Fleet Street, gathered a huge team of the star journalists
of post-war Britain and cared little for profits. His paper was all about
news. Today journalism is about culling gossip from Facebook and
Twitter, chasing celebrities, providing endless opinionated and tedious

comment, particularly about politics, and of course snide reporting of the lives and deficiencies of ordinary people. I abandoned any respect for David Cameron when he tried to restrict the scope of the Leveson Enquiry into the culture, practices and ethics of the press.

I shall return to Michael as the honest journalist that he was when I look at his background and early history, but on this occasion I want to turn away from my subject's career in journalism and concentrate on what for him became an abiding passion, his major contribution to conservation, and especially to the worldwide conservation of the salmon, working with his friend and colleague, the Icelander Orri Vigfússon. Orri died in 2017 but his legacy, as Chairman of the North Atlantic Salmon Fund, will continue.

I first met Michael when he was part of a tiny fishing syndicate on the River Erme in Devon. He tells me that my catch of eight sea trout one night probably remains the record for the river! He and his friends were ardent sea trout fishermen but they also wanted to find some salmon fishing that was less crowded than most angling association waters. They heard that the best stretches on the River Lynher in Cornwall might be for sale through John Foot, a solicitor in Plymouth. John, who became a Liberal peer, was one of five talented sons of Isaac Foot, an ardent Methodist, a Liberal Party firebrand and founder of the family law firm in Plymouth. Isaac's most famous son was Michael Foot, the former leader of the Labour Party.

Isaac Foot lived in a big house in the valley on the River Lynher and owned around 1,000 acres of good farmland. In the 1930s' agricultural depression he sold the land but, surprisingly, retained the fishing and shooting rights on the estate. Michael Foot often told me in Parliament of his childhood in this river valley and its beauty and isolation.

The celebrated fishing author Augustus Grimble described the Lynher as the best fishing river in Cornwall before it was utterly destroyed by arsenic effluent from the Cornish mines. When five of us bought Isaac Foot's stretch of the river about two miles long for a total of £4,100 in 1964 the mining had ceased and the salmon and sea trout were returning to spawn in the upper river. Indeed, in the first years it was possible to see as many as twenty salmon and big sea trout in separate pools on the river. The commercial nets were taking 450 salmon a year in 1972 and the rod catch for the river was 245. Subsequently, John Foot gave us freehold shooting rights over about 600 acres of woods and farmland.

Now I am conscious that many readers of this book will know nothing of fishing – and will have no particular wish to learn more – but I must explain that the iconic Atlantic salmon is one of the most threatened species in the natural world. Its future survival is challenged today by overfishing, by changes in its Atlantic feedstock, by global warming and the retreating Arctic ice.

When the Atlantic salmon leaves the river as a young smolt it has to travel to its rich feeding grounds off Greenland and the Faroe Islands and there it puts on nearly all its weight. Most UK salmon return to their home rivers to spawn after a year's eating and voyaging at sea, but some, known as multi-sea winter salmon, stay in the ocean for several years and may grow to 50 or 60lb or more before returning home.

The large fall in salmon numbers in recent times and a drop in their average size has inspired many salmon enthusiasts to try to arrest the decline. To illustrate just how radically the salmon's fortunes have changed I can give an example from the 1950s. From the first pool on the River Exe, known as Salmon Pool, Colonel Steve Church, the agent of Lord Devon, and my sister's husband, Major Parker, sometimes used to catch up to forty salmon a day in the early spring season. Their haul was collected daily by a MacFisheries van! The annual rod catch for the entire River Exe in 2016 amounted to only 124 salmon.

Nobody lavished more of his time and money on saving the Atlantic salmon than Orri Vigfússon, an Icelandic businessman and entrepreneur; and Michael Charleston devoted much of his retirement to helping him. Orri, who came from a traditional herring-fishing family, saw Iceland's herring fishery vanish as a result of overfishing and feared that the Atlantic salmon would go the same way. With the help of several of his Icelandic angling friends he took up the challenge and launched the North Atlantic Salmon Fund (NASF). Michael and Orri worked together very closely on endless media campaigns, arguing with governments on both sides of the Atlantic.

The fund, by dint of Vigfússon devoting most of his life to NASF from 1989 until his death in 2017, and campaigning internationally against the folly of governments continuing to allow commercial fisheries to plunder the shrunken Atlantic salmon stocks, has raised many millions of dollars and pounds, mainly from wealthy fishing enthusiasts, to compensate professional fishermen who agree to stop salmon fishing and switch to other kinds of fish that are sustainable.

The Atlantic salmon's vast saltwater range lies north of a line that could be drawn from northern Spain to New England on America's eastern seaboard. Mainly as a result of Orri's zeal and negotiating skills, and the entirely voluntary work of the many people he recruited to help him, within that area the salmon is now largely protected from commercial exploitation. The exceptions remain in Norway's big Finnmark fishery that kills 60 to 70 per cent of the spring salmon heading for Russian rivers, a reduced coastal fishery off North East England and parts of Scotland.

Most importantly, within the 200-mile limits off Greenland and the Faroe Islands, salmon swim and feed largely in safety. Orri brought this about by persuasion and by compensating salmon fishing families for the loss of their livelihood. With NASF's help, many Greenlanders switched to an entirely new caviar-style industry that exports lumpfish roes. Later the Irish government banned the sea netting of salmon off the coast of Ireland. All of this has made a major contribution to saving the Atlantic salmon from possible extinction.

Unfortunately, in the United Kingdom we have been dogged over many years by the incompetence of the Environment Agency, whose extensive remit extends from nuclear safety to the protection of elvers. Given its vast range of responsibilities, it is not surprising that the small team in Whitehall that oversees salmon conservation is the most ineffective and bureaucratic in the otherwise talented civil service. It is obsessed by control and with its diminishing resources and staff it clings on to its authority with grim determination.

In the old days, responsibility for conservation lay with the local river boards. The Cornwall River Board consisted of fishermen, farmers and local councillors. It relied on their practical knowledge of the rivers: it followed the marine scientists with care and scepticism. It worked on the ground, not from Whitehall.

The salmon has continued to decline in many rivers, and as a result increasing interest has been shown by anglers in the creation of local hatcheries. The Environment Agency has closed all its hatcheries and regards local hatcheries with haughty scepticism.

The most dramatic example of hatchery success is the River Tyne, where the once huge salmon rod and net catches – up to 129,100 in 1873 – collapsed to nil from industrial pollution in the river and the estuary at Newcastle. When the Kielder Water reservoir was created in the 1980s the water authorities agreed to establish the Kielder hatchery to replace the 160,000 salmon parr (juveniles) scientists reckoned could have been born annually in the Tyne headwaters drowned under the reservoir.

A hatchery genius, Peter Gray, became its first superintendent. Under his management and through his observation and experiment the output of the hatchery grew to 1.2 million salmon parr annually by 1979 to 1983. He released most of them into the Tyne and, as a result of this unique experiment and the removal of most of the river's pollution, the Tyne rod catch has gone from nothing to an annual average over the past ten years of 3,000 salmon, the highest rod catch in England and Wales. Peter Gray went on to develop a hatchery in New England and another in Devon on the River Tamar. But his West Country work was frustrated by delays in obtaining water abstraction and discharge licences from the Environment Agency. It failed.

In 2011, Michael Charleston, together with Peter Gray, of whom he was a friend and a great supporter (Gray had his critics), published *Swimming Against the Tide*, the definitive book on the resurrection of the River Tyne. It has become the bible of small hatcheries in Scotland and elsewhere in England.

In Cornwall, we have run a small local hatchery on the River Lynher for the past ten years. We don't mark our parr on release so we have no firm evidence that hatchery-reared parr are successful beside the naturally spawned fish in the river, but with the permission of the Environment Agency we catch eight hens and eight cocks each year and hold the fish in our tanks until we are ready to strip their eggs and milt, normally in December/January (see the chapter on Ted Hughes). The fish are then returned to the river. All this voluntary work takes place in the garden and under the guidance of Nick Lintott with the assistance of Arthur White, Graham Hake and Paul Muggeridge, all volunteers who give their time for nothing.

We release up to 50,000 fry annually. Do they survive? We don't know. But I find it difficult to believe that a very small percentage do not find their way to the distant feeding grounds and return to spawn in their native river. There have been difficulties – pump breakdowns, flooding and overheated river temperature, possibly due to global warming. We have discovered water temperature is key, as Michael and Peter Gray emphasize in their book. At the time of writing we have held back 15,000 fry to grow to about six inches long. They will be planted out in late autumn when the native brown trout are thinking about sex rather than eating baby salmon. We hope that up to 10 per cent of the release will survive to return to the river as mature spawners after their feeding trip to Greenland and elsewhere. The latest news is that the catch on our two miles of the little River Lynher in 2017 amounted to 49 salmon and around 120 sea trout. It must be due to our hatchery.

I conclude this chapter by talking of Michael Charleston's personal journey. He was born in Penzance, a few miles from Land's End. His father was a market gardener, growing vegetables in a large field at Long Rock. Michael won a scholarship to Penzance Grammar School. His ambition was to become a Merchant Navy officer, so naturally he joined the local Sea Cadets. The Second World War was an exciting time for teenagers, especially if one was a sea cadet in Penzance.

When Michael retired from journalism it was thought that he would make an ideal campaigning secretary for the South West Rivers Association. With the enthusiastic support of many of the riparian owners who were the backbone of the fishing community, Michael began a long effort to get the management of the game fish rivers of England and Wales returned to the hands of the local people who knew and loved them best. His eloquent arguments and publicity work soon attracted the attention of the river associations elsewhere in England and in Wales, the vast majority of which were equally despairing of the failure of the Environment Agency to fulfil its statutory duty 'to maintain, improve and develop salmon and freshwater fisheries in England and Wales'.

Michael's plan to revive the river boards was not adopted by the government; too many jobs would have been lost in the Environment Agency. But today the various river trusts, following the lead of the West Country River Trust – a creation of the South West Rivers

Association – have taken over much of the work the Environment Agency was supposed to do. Michael says: 'For years I thought we'd failed but today, thanks to the trusts, I suppose we have accomplished much of what we tried to get.' He was awarded an OBE in 2004 for his conservation work.

At school Michael's future was always marked out as the Merchant Navy. In 1945 its officer training first involved a year at sea at the age of sixteen, followed by two years at nautical college. When Michael was told so many ships had been lost that it would be six to nine months before a berth at sea became available he reluctantly accepted his headmaster's advice to try for a reporting vacancy on the local paper, as a temporary stopgap.

His journalistic career took off from there, culminating in thirty very successful years with the old broadsheet *Daily Express*. I met him many times over several decades, during which time he showed complete integrity in his reporting, not least when he was leading the *Daily Express* team covering the Falklands War. I trusted him completely. It is a good story. It is, however, as a conservationist of the salmon that he will be remembered. He is a hero – no doubt about it.

Chapter Ten

Ted Hughes

Poet Laureate

T ed was absolutely brilliant – his literary output is astonishing – but I didn't appreciate it when I knew him. We went on many fishing expeditions together but I don't recall us talking much about poetry or literature. We might have talked about Ted's passion for Shakespeare or Ovid, but we didn't. We might have mentioned his famous poems 'The River', 'Pike', 'Thrushes', 'The Hawk in the Rain', but we didn't. Why?

I realize now that fishing was an escape for Ted. He was a poet escaping from his wide circle of admirers and two ghastly tragedies in his earlier life. Ted said in an interview: 'When I am fishing alone, as I come out of it, if I have to speak to somebody, I find I can't speak properly. I can't form words. The words sort of come out backwards, tumbled. It takes time to re-adjust, as if I'd been in some part of myself that pre-dates language.'

He lost himself fishing, with nature and in a river. This sketch may disappoint some, because it is about Ted the man, not his poetry. On my side I was a politician escaping the drudgery and media abuse often suffered by all members of the profession. Both of us were passionately committed to our work, but it is impossible to be a celebrated poet or a politician without some means of escape, in our case an obsession with rivers and the nature which accompanied them. As Ted's obituary in the *Independent* said, following his death in October 1998: 'The papers will be full of Ted Hughes this weekend. Ted the literary genius, Ted Poet Laureate, Ted ex-husband of Sylvia Plath. But I never knew him as any of these things very much. To me, Ted Hughes was much more interesting than just being a poet. Ted was a fisherman.'

Ted and I never said much to each other, except to discuss the fly we were using, which fish rushed to the fly and spat it out, what we saw and experienced on the river bank, the wonderful Scottish ghillies, when they were sober. I realize, on reflection, how our early lives, although completely different, embraced a similar love of nature and rivers. Ted with the Rochdale canal beside the now demolished Zion Chapel in the Yorkshire Pennines, where he would catch little sticklebacks and put them in a 2lb jam jar on the kitchen windowsill. Next morning they would all be dead – that's what boys do. Once, under the canal bridge, there was even a leaping trout.

In his reading of 'The Canal's Drowning Black' on radio, Hughes said that the trout had 'a magical meaning for me'. It was an 'authentic aboriginal . . . the holiest creature out there in its free unspoiled sacred world'. It was the precursor of all the salmon which later came to embody for him the whole life-to-death-to-new-life adventure.

The significance of wild nature was not only directly experienced by the young Hughes, but also mediated to him by his boyhood reading. Around their campfires on the moor, Ted and his older brother Gerald would discuss the wonders they read about in books.

Ted is not easy to understand, nor is his poetry easy to follow.

For me, in early youth, life existed in the rivers Taw and Torridge, the two rivers described in Henry Williamson's two brilliant books, *Salar the Salmon* and *Tarka the Otter*. Both of us quite independently loved these books. When Ted moved with Sylvia Plath to Devon he lived with and through these same two great rivers in their new home at North Tawton.

Through our mutual friend Simon Day we were both introduced to the personalities and grandees of the West Country. When we went fishing together in Scotland on the Tay, Naver and Spey, Devon was the topic of much of our conversation, never poetry or literature. An extract from *Letters* explains how we met:

To Gerald and Joan Hughes

16 December 1986

Did you like the casual bit, Gerald, about Squadron Leaders and Air Vice Marshals? . . . Strange world – a world of social revelations, X-rays of England's anatomy, encephelograms of

England's brain, this world of retired high ranking servicemen. But I get on with them. Apart from the . . . N.W. frontier speech systems, many of them are remarkable chaps, naturally enough. Also, without them, I fancy there'd be no Salmon rivers left at all. The shooting – in which I seem to have lost all interest – belongs to the Bankers, Landed Rich, & Company directors – plus a few rich farmers. We have a whole gang of them that we sometimes play with – I've got to know them mainly through one of them who invited me to join his consortium when he made a bid for the South West T.V. franchise . . . He owns the best and most beautiful bit of the river Dart – and that was his bribe. So we became fishing pals – then his wife and Carol became close friends. And now, it seems, we're knit together with knots. Through him I got to know a whole procession of those figures for whom you used to breed pheasants. Simon's (this pal of mine) father often shot at Alphington. Also through him I've met a troop of Tory politicians. I've got to know some better, since they get tangled into our fishing trips. A scatter of Lords – Courtenay down at Powderham Castle (on the Exe, you remember) & Clinton. So it's a mighty peculiar box sea view I have of this particular theatre of play. Mainly I meet them at feasts – at Simon's – and on fishing jams. They know how to enjoy their lives, I must say. In fact, Simon introduced me to that whole army of occupation – invisible, pretty well, to the common Englander, except . . . stormy voices in the House of Parliament. A very fascinating education (for what?) for me, you can guess.

Although Ted became a close friend of the Queen Mother and Prince Charles, he was always the son of a carpenter, curious and amused about the world into which Simon Day introduced him. He was relaxed with royals, aristocrats, politicians; perhaps less so with his doting fan club who reminded him of Sylvia Plath. I attended his memorial service in Westminster Abbey before his recognition in Poets' Corner – and there seemed to be more attractive women than men in attendance!

I have got to understand Ted better after he died through the critic and his friend, the late Keith Sagar. I quote quite extensively from the work set out in his website. He said of Ted that possibly his greatest poem was 'River': 'It seems to me not only Hughes's finest collection, but one of the greatest books of world literature.'

> The poems in 'River' are arranged almost exactly to follow the cycle of the year, from salmon-stripping in late December to the spawning in the following January. In his interview Hughes recalled a dream of walking by a big, swift river:

> > And coming up this river were these big salmon. As they came past me they were leaping. And as they leapt they shook themselves in the air. As they shook themselves in the air, their milt and spawn were splashed over me. I was completely covered with milt and spawn from these leaping salmon.

> > Keith Sagar, *Autobiography*

In 'The Morning Before Christmas' Hughes and seven other men at the salmon ladder perform the 'precarious obstetrics' of stripping first hen salmon of their eggs, then cock salmon of their milt, into plastic bowls, then solemnly, lovingly, perform the lavings and drainings and re-washing, in an effort to improve slightly the terrible odds against survival.

> The current hosing over their brows and shoulders,
> Bellies riven open and shaken empty
> Into the gutter of pebbles
> In an orgy of eggs and sperm
> The dance orgy of being reborn.

The life of the salmon is the life of the living waters, sea and river, which is the life of earth and sky, which is our only life. The salmon is part of a flow which 'will not let up for a minute'. The river is itself an archetypal image of life in time, a process which Eliot had described as the one-way helpless journey towards death. But a river is by no means a one-way wastage.

In the first edition of *River*, the sequence of poems published in 1983, the collection, says Sagar, is framed by the two poems beginning with

'The Morning Before Christmas' and ending with 'Salmon Eggs'. This emphasis on birth does not discount death, for death is the price to be paid for birth. Birth in the opening poem is set in a context where the odds are 'five thousand to one against survival', and the lucky few are 'dead within days of marriage'.

Life in *River* is 'the bliss of making and unmaking', unmaking in order to continue the cycle of making. In 'Salmon Eggs' the mating salmon are 'emptying themselves for each other'. This selfless giving is a form of dedication or worship. The ending is the October salmon's slow death. The spent salmon, worn out with his 2,000-mile journey, 'earth's insatiable quest', ends as a 'shroud in a gutter' – 'this chamber of horrors is also home'.

Even his dead body is needed, as food for scavengers, and to provide essential nutrients for the rainforest, on which depend the rains which will make it possible for the next generation of salmon to reach their upstream spawning grounds. All creatures but man are part of this machinery, which he seems intent on dismantling.

It is all quite difficult, and for those who are not fishermen, or are not spiritually awed by rivers, it can seem very strange and eccentric. But surely one must admire a man who wrote this great poetry, endless children's stories and dissected Shakespeare and Ovid, but thought mainly of rivers.

How Ted had the energy and time to pour out all this literature and also travel the world to explore rivers from British Columbia to Alaska is remarkable. Even down to the most modest chalk streams and especially Devon's Taw and Torridge, which both of us saw as almost sacred rivers.

I think he captured what he felt when he wrote in a letter to Keith Sagar about a visit to Alaska:

Alaska was everything I'd hoped. Everything happened I wanted to happen, & a whole lot more. We caught salmon until we were actually sick of catching them. We got ourselves off great lakes (living time, 5 minutes of immersion – so cold) by the skin of our teeth two or 3 times. We fished alongside bears. Lay awake listening to wolves. And generally sleepwalked through that dreamland. Unearthly valleys of flowers between snow mountains. Miles of purple lupins.

So I conclude by quoting from Keith Sagar again writing about 'Ted Hughes: Visionary':

Ted Hughes was born in 1930 in Mytholmroyd, deep in the Calder Valley of West Yorkshire. Though he later described the area as 'the cradle of the industrial revolution in textiles', it was not difficult to escape into woods or onto the high moors. He claimed that for him in childhood the word 'horizon' was the most magical in the language. His much older brother initiated him into the natural world by taking him as retriever on his hunting excursions. The split between the world of men and industry and the world of wild nature was particularly stark here, and imprinted itself on Hughes' psyche. Poetry came to seem for him the voice of wild nature trying to make itself heard above the cacophony of mills, schools and churches. It seemed to him an extension of fishing.

Nevertheless he found himself 'in the cooker' of grammar school and university, the intellectual, academic life, and soon after married another poet, Sylvia Plath, whose work was dedicated, at first to fame and success. The responsibility of providing for wife and children tied Hughes securely to that world. Otherwise, he wrote, he would have been fishing in a boat off Western Australia.

From his school days Hughes was greatly attracted to myth and folklore. His English master's leaving present from Mexborough Grammar School was a copy of Robert Graves' *The White Goddess*, which replaced Henry Williamson's *Tarka the Otter* as his sacred book.

Hughes described his early poems as bulletins from the constant battle between vitality and death. From the first poem in his first book *The Hawk in the Rain* (1957) he was aware how tenuously and briefly life maintains its foothold against Death.

I remember one of the few occasions outside our fishing expeditions when Ted and I talked about poetry and myth; it was when I told him that I had recently seen the great painting by Titian, *Diana and Actaeon*, in the National Gallery. He reminded me of his poem about Diana in his book *Tales from Ovid*. Surely this great poem describes Ted more fully than in many of his other works. I have had to shorten it:

For Actaeon. It is no crime
To lose your way in a dark wood.

It happened on a mountain where hunters
Had slaughtered so many animals
The slopes were patched red with the butchering places.

When Shadows were shortest and the sun's heat hardest
Young Actaeon called a halt:
We have killed more than enough for the day.
All concurred . . .

Making a beeline home from the hunt
Stumbled on this gorge. Surprised to find it,
He pushed into it, apprehensive, but
Steered by a pitiless fate – whose nudging he felt
Only as surges of curiosity.

He peered
Into the gloom to see the waterfall –
But what he saw were nymphs, their wild faces
Screaming at him in a commotion of water.
And as his eyes adjusted, he saw they were naked,
Beating their breasts as they screamed at him.
And he saw they were crowding together
To hide something from him. He stared harder.
Those nymphs could not conceal Diana's whiteness,
The tallest barely reached her navel. Actaeon
Stared at the goddess, who stared at him.
She twisted her breasts away, showing him her back.
Glaring at him over her shoulder
She blushed like a dawn cloud . . .

No weapon was to hand – only water.
So she scooped up a handful and dashed it
Into his astonished eyes, as she shouted:
'Now, if you can, tell how you saw me naked.'
That was all she said, but as she said it
Out of his forehead burst a rack of antlers.
His neck lengthened, narrowed, and his ears
Folded to whiskery points, his hands were hooves,
His arms long slender legs. His hunter's tunic
Slid from his dappled hide. With all this
The goddess
Poured a shocking stream of panic terror
Through his heart like blood. Actaeon
Bounded out across the cave's pool
In plunging leaps, amazed at his own lightness.
And there
Clear in the bulging mirror of his bow-wave
He glimpsed his antlered head,
And cried: 'What has happened to me?'
The first to give tongue were Melampus
And the deep-thinking Ichnobates . . .

The whole pack piled in after . . .

Too many to name. The strung-out pack,
Locked onto their quarry.
Where Actaeon had so often strained
Every hound to catch and kill the quarry,
Now he strained to shake the same hounds off –
His own hounds. He tried to cry out:
'I am Actaeon – remember your master,' . . .

Every hound filled its jaws . . .

The terrible method
of his murderers, as they knotted

Muscles and ferocity to dismember
Their own master.
Only when Actaeon's life
Had been torn from his bones, to the last mouthful,
Only then
Did the remorseless anger of Diana,
Goddess of the arrow, find peace.

There it all is. Diana and her naked nymphs. The bloodthirsty hunt. Actaeon with his hounds. Cursed by Diana, he is turned into a stag himself and is torn to pieces by his own hounds. The remorseless anger of Diana has had her revenge.

So much of Ted's poetry is based on myth, on violence, on death and rebirth, on the life of the salmon. And yet, as a fellow fisherman, I knew him as a calm and thoughtful being, although, dare I say it, I think Diana was in truth Sylvia Plath gaining her revenge for Ted's infidelity.

Sagar continued:

Hughes felt that after the death of Sylvia, the rest of his life would be posthumous. But he found a great healing resource in fishing, which became almost a religion. To enter water and become continuous through his rod and line with the holy life of that magical element was a form of atonement.

In 1970 he had married a farmer's daughter, Carol Orchard, and in 1972 he bought Moortown Farm in Devon and ran it with Carol and her father until Jack Orchard's death in 1976. Farming literally brought Hughes down to earth after his excursions into prophetic books. It proved, for all the frustrations and losses, extremely therapeutic. From a world of blood he found himself baptised into a world of mud, of life at its most grounded in the land, animal life and the seasons. It bred in him the conviction that 'only birth matters'. Without that experience it is unlikely that Hughes would have come through to write his finest pastoral elegies, *Moortown Diary*, *Remains of Elmet* and *River*.

Chapter Eleven

Lord Heseltine

Politician

I arrived a few minutes late for my lunch at Buck's Club with Michael Heseltine. He was seated in a corner of the dining room: 'They put me in Churchill's chair,' he said with a smile – of course they did, and so they should have done! Margaret Thatcher said of him, 'The trouble with Michael is that he suffers from "terminal charisma".'

As I was talking to him a thought occurred to me: he should have been smacked quite hard by his nanny in his early youth and told that you cannot always get your own way in life, nor can you always come out on top.

Michael has nearly always got his own way in life. He came out on top but not as he would define it. He has achieved what most people would feel was success, fame, fortune and public recognition; by that I mean people know who he is. Only the last honour defeated him, the office of Prime Minister.

Michael was the hero of the party members at the annual Conservative Conference. He was a great performer; together with other MPs I hated the Conference and always avoided Michael's rumbustious speeches. The famous parliamentary sketch writer Frank Johnson gave an amusing description of a Heseltine performance:

> One arrived to find Mr Heseltine engulfed in his own peroration. A huge audience was enthralled. He bellowed at them from beneath that blond mane which causes him so often to be mistaken from behind for Mrs Sally Oppenheim. He was thundering along the lines of 'one nation, one Reich, one Heseltine'.

Michael and I entered Parliament at the same time in 1966, and he followed me as a Secretary of State for Trade and then Defence. I left Parliament early, he stayed on and became Deputy Prime Minister under

John Major. Over many years he has been a friend of mine, and although we are 'ideological opposites', as I said in a message to him, we have never had a cross word. And if our political friendship proves anything, it is that the Conservative Party is a very broad church.

I was thinking also that the two Parliamentarians of my generation who stood out from the aspiring crowd as being special were Michael Heseltine and Kenneth Clarke. Both stood for the Party leadership and were defeated, quite decisively. How can that be, when in my opinion they were more talented and interesting than John Major, David Cameron or Theresa May? I do not criticize these three Prime Ministers in any way at all; a gap opened up, sometimes out of nowhere, and they were all sufficiently opportunistic to grab the crown – leaving two more exceptional men behind . . . politics is an unfair world.

I said that Michael and I were 'ideological opposites', so we sat down and tried to define what divided us. We went through the silly labels used by lazy journalists like 'wet and dry', 'left wing and right wing', 'Whig versus Tory', but they seemed inappropriate, not least because we agreed on so many things. We both favoured competition in markets against protectionism. We sympathized with the traumas suffered by thousands of good people as a result of the decline of the coal, shipbuilding and steel industries. But neither of us would have kept those industries going indefinitely with subsidy. We both favoured an economic policy that ensured that the country lived within its means; we both favoured strong defence, including a nuclear deterrent under tight budgetary control. We both strongly favoured the sale of council houses, a great policy under Michael's direction at Environment. Finally, I do not think that either of us would have neglected the first duty of government to support the poor and disadvantaged with welfare – although the means and measure of how government did so would always be debatable.

It is not difficult to understand how we could have served on endless Cabinet committees under Margaret Thatcher's chairmanship, particularly when he was at Environment, without much disagreement on principles, even if maybe here and there on detail.

Even now, when our disagreement on the European Union is passionate and intense, there has not been any slanging match in public. Sometimes I wish he would take a break from television and media appearances, but I think he has conducted his campaign against the government with dignity, if not restraint, in contrast to George Osborne, who has behaved like a spoilt child; indeed, it was Osborne's absurd hyperbole that drove so many into the 'Leave' camp.

Currently, Michael is hopelessly overexposed and is doing his cause no service. Sometimes he seems to be in a celebrity contest with Paris Hilton and President Trump. What I find especially irritating in both Heseltine and Clarke is their repeated calumny that all those seeking a recovery of British sovereignty are 'right wing'. What is right wing or left wing about the seventeen million people who voted to leave the European Union? Seventeen million voted to take back control from an unelected bureaucracy in Brussels and a politically motivated European Court of Justice. For some of the fifty years since we joined the Common Market the Labour Party, and not least its present leader, Mr Corbyn, has been a staunch opponent of European integration. Is Mr Corbyn right wing? It is a silly charge against people who happen to disagree with Europhiles like Heseltine and Clarke.

I was horrified when Theresa May asked Michael to step down from the valuable voluntary work that he had been undertaking in No. 10 about the cities without speaking to him personally; her decision was put to him by the Chief Whip in the House of Lords. It was a classic case of insensitivity and poor man management – that sort of behaviour places a question mark over Theresa's May's ability to hold down the job. Why, too, did she need to create a rift with George Osborne by being gratuitously rude to him?

So we agreed to plod through old government issues to identify our differences; that was difficult, too. Michael reminded me of a right royal punch-up we had with Margaret Thatcher over what now seems as a relatively trivial issue: the building of the Queen Elizabeth II Conference Centre opposite Westminster Abbey. Margaret was determined, with Treasury support, to block it. Each time we met to discuss it, she refused to sum up the meeting. So it came back for decision three times, when eventually Michael and I won out over a stubborn Prime Minister. 'You see,' said Michael, 'we agreed!'

He reminded me of the nationalization of Rolls-Royce when he was Aerospace Minister under Ted Heath. Surely, he said, you must have opposed it. No, I said, it was inevitable. I was a Treasury Minister and I supported it. I went up to Ted Heath in the voting lobby and said, 'Prime Minister, I think that you did the right thing, you had no choice.' Ted scarcely acknowledged my support; he had a barely disguised contempt for his junior ministers.

Then we remembered the famous occasion when Michael persuaded Margaret Thatcher to hold a major seminar in No. 10 to persuade the Whitehall establishment of Michael's pet subject MINIS, a means of identifying inefficiencies in ministries and employing his mission to root out waste in departments. She invited all the Permanent Secretaries and several senior ministers to a large gathering. Michael made his splurge, with loyal nodding and agreement among the assembled mandarins – they wanted to keep their jobs! Margaret then went round the room asking for support for Michael's proposals. There was wide agreement. She then turned to me and said MINIS was badly required in the Ministry of Defence.

I said, 'Prime Minister, I am sure it would be valuable to save some money in my department but I do not have the time to spend on MINIS when I am grappling with billions of pounds of overspending and defence equipment inflation running at over 18 per cent.'

The Prime Minister was furious. The mandarins loved it, of course, and the meeting ended in some disarray. We both had a good laugh at the memory. Government must be fun or it could be misery.

So why, in spite of my liking and admiration for Michael's achievements in business and getting things done in government, do I admit that I could never have voted for him as leader of the Conservative Party? My personal friendship has never stood in the way of my distaste for his political philosophy.

First, I am not sure that Michael is a Conservative, or my kind of Conservative. Maybe he is a Whig and I am a Tory. I think he is a 'liberal activist'. There's nothing wrong with that. He was an excellent Minister, especially during his several years as Secretary of State for the Environment – that department needed a real doer – and his achievement in Docklands and in our northern cities was remarkable. In the broad church that is the Conservative Party he provided balance and energy, particularly when it came to resisting some of the more outlandish behaviour of Margaret Thatcher.

In Thatcher's first government Michael could never have been described as a 'wet'. He did not support the protests of Carrington, Gilmour, Pym, St John Stevas, Prior, Soames and others at Thatcher's economic policy. The Cabinet was riven with disagreement, but Michael kept out of it. He did not speak up for Geoffrey Howe, the Chancellor, but I do not remember that he ever opposed the very difficult and uncomfortable measures that the government had to take at that time.

Why did the Party, particularly the MPs, fail to support his candidature at the critical time following Margaret Thatcher's resignation? Of course Europe was a main reason, but not the only one. I think there was always nervousness about allowing his hand on the tiller, the sense of risk that would accompany it. He surely showed that the parliamentary electorate was correct when they saw his frantic behaviour over the Westland issue in 1985.

Interestingly, although Ken Clarke also ruled himself out on Europe, he would have been seen as a steadier hand and would have represented less risk than his colleague. When John Major, Douglas Hurd and Michael Heseltine stood for the leadership, Margaret Thatcher, in a typically cutting remark, said the parliamentary electorate were offered a poor choice of candidates! If so, it was her fault and no one else's. In my view, however, Margaret was correct in one respect. The Major government for me, dominated by Hurd as Foreign Secretary, Clarke as Chancellor and Heseltine as Deputy Prime Minister, was something of a disaster. I was one of Major's 'bastards' when I joined the Maastricht rebels; that should have been the moment to stop the Common Market turning into the European Union with its federalist ambitions.

So back to our differences. Leaving Europe to one side, what is the philosophy that divides us? It surely must be industrial policy. Michael is a corporatist; he is a traditional Whig; he defers to big business. I am suspicious of big business; I am a traditional Tory. At the crisis meeting over Geoffrey Howe's proposal for further cuts in government expenditure which I describe in my sketch of Margaret Thatcher he actually proposed a return to Prices and Incomes Policy. It is indicative of his belief in government's ability to foster and restore prosperity. When we met, he told me that he was preparing a leaflet on 'Industrial Policy' in answer to the government's forthcoming

White Paper on that subject. I groaned inwardly. Here we go again. Politicians and civil servants assisting the market; normally second-guessing the market and trying to push it along with their prejudices and ambitious ideas.

I read his own paper on Industrial Policy with care. It is well argued and made the point that, with 40 per cent of our economy within the public sector, it is inevitable that all governments are irretrievably sucked into making decisions about industrial 'issues'; but that is a wholly different world from an overarching 'policy' for industry.

I spent some of my time in the City engaged in what is known as 'Private Equity'; I was an adviser to Apax, one of the most successful firms in developing new business. Michael's leaflet was correct in saying that new company formation, greatly encouraged, I must say, by Gordon Brown when Chancellor, has been a notable success in this country. The entrepreneurial spirit is there. The problem is moving small and successful companies into the next stage of growth before their owners sell out and retire to their yachts and second houses. There is a cultural problem with the English and business. Part of the problem lies in our ludicrous estate duties, which discourage the growth of family-controlled businesses that are, for instance, Germany's greatest strength. I do not understand what governments can do to support growth from small to medium-sized business, other than encourage them through the tax system.

Michael agrees, I think, that government is normally to be discouraged from 'picking winners'. It was not successful in the 1970s and 1980s, but how do you avoid it, if you have an 'Industrial Policy'?

In his leaflet he also argues that government is a huge influence on business through its procurement; nowhere is this more evident than in the Ministry of Defence. Both of us were directly involved in making decisions to spend hundreds of millions of pounds on defence equipment, but I never saw this as part of an industrial strategy.

Indeed, I hesitated before agreeing to the planning of a new fighter aircraft at Wharton when it had run out of work on the Tornado. Were we correct to sustain the British aerospace industry when it was in danger of foundering for lack of work? I think so. It was a purely pragmatic decision and had nothing to do with any industrial policy.

My hesitation on strategic grounds at that juncture at the height of the Cold War was because it was Germany's role in NATO, not ours, to develop and finance an agile fighter aircraft for continental defence. Our contribution to NATO, with our limited resources, would have been better concentrated on our naval/air task in the North Atlantic.

But my move to sustain Wharton with a new design led Michael to go on and create the European fighter aircraft (now the Typhoon), which he successfully developed into a cooperative multi-national European programme. It has been an expensive success but, again, it has nothing to do with an industrial policy.

Unfortunately, it led to his determination to force a European solution on Westland when its board and the market favoured an American investment. It led to the resignation of Leon Brittan, the Trade Secretary, and dangerously undermined the Prime Minister's authority. It was a good example of a Minister second-guessing the market to meet his pure ideological objectives – that is exactly the danger for Ministers possessed of an industrial policy.

Since I embarked on this subject, the government has published its own proposals for an Industrial Policy, Command 9528. It runs to more than 250 pages, but at the end of it I am unable to detect any coherent understanding of what constitutes growth in a developed economy. It is clearly correct in emphasizing the vital importance of productivity, but that is more about industrial culture, a relaxed regulatory regime and education than picking victims for government support. It is ultimately a PR exercise for business and designed to please the CBI; it is easier to say that the government has an industrial policy than to say that it doesn't. The government has picked four 'winners': electric cars, artificial intelligence, clean growth and an ageing society. You can be sure that some 'winners' will probably fail. The foundations to growth are listed as ideas, people and infrastructure, of course, but that is not an industrial policy, it is a statement of the obvious. You can be sure that every large company member of the CBI will now be in a queue at the Business Department seeking taxpayers' money for their own pet schemes – barging out of the way the small and medium-sized companies which are bound to be the generators of tomorrow's winners. Can you imagine the Business Department in Whitehall removing itself to California and picking Google, Facebook and Amazon as tomorrow's winners? None of them were the consequence of US government industrial policy.

So where does that leave Michael Heseltine, passionately keen on kick-starting the British economy into a new world of economic growth and entrepreneurial adventure? He seems to prefer the sclerotic bureaucracy and protectionism represented by the European Union, with its stranglehold on trade. The European Union and a successful British industrial policy are in stark opposition to each other.

However, I wish Michael well! He is energetic, determined and a 'believer' – so much better than just going along with the consensus of the day.

Chapter Twelve

Billy Collins

Cornish farmer

When my wife and I first bought our farm, Trewinnard, in Cornwall in 1975, we were surrounded by small farmers. A minority, perhaps, were tenants of the three big landlords in the area: the St Aubyns of St Michael's Mount, the Bolithos of Trengwainton near Penzance and Lord Falmouth of Tregothnan near Truro. But the greater number were single family-owned holdings of around fifty acres. Our neighbour Billy Collins assists us on our farm today. The son of a local farmer himself, he appears to me inseparable from the land; in this essay I therefore afford myself the luxury of combining the subject of farming in Cornwall – close to my heart – with a salute to a notable individual who has devoted all his life to that occupation and who has been successful in rapidly changing times.

Billy's grandfather was a gardener at St Michael's Mount, and when he told Lord St Levan (St Aubyn) of his wish to farm, his generous and paternalistic employer give him twelve acres of land overlooking Mount's Bay. He worked on the roads to supplement his income and was given access to a quarry, where he took responsibility for blasting road stone.

When Billy's father took over in 1956 he was farming fifty-two acres, and Billy followed his father after leaving school. I first met them when they purchased an old combine harvester and supplemented their income by harvesting crops on neighbouring farms, including ours. The grain was only used as cattle feed for the twelve farmers in Marazion parish, all of whom are now gone.

Slowly, over the years, Billy purchased extra land and rented more where he could. Back in 1968 they had twenty cows and were growing twenty acres of cauliflower, which all went to local shops via wholesale markets. This market gardening was made possible by the frost-free land overlooking Mount's Bay – and they avoided the disease of brassicas called club root by dressing the land regularly with seaweed from the adjoining beach, and sand.

Billy made an interesting observation when he told me that seaweed is in poor supply today. He speculated as to whether this was due to pollution of the seabed by chemicals following the nearby *Torrey Canyon* oil tanker disaster of 1967, or more likely from the absence of sewage in the sea following the establishment of sewage farms on land.

Today he is farming around 500 acres, which includes our farm of around 180 acres, and he is combining up to 700 acres with two modern combine harvesters for neighbouring farmers. As a former businessman, I am appalled when I visit his farmyard and see what must amount to over £1 million worth of tractors, harvesters, cold stores and equipment! The farm is entirely a family enterprise; there is no outside labour apart from the six piecework labourers from Eastern Europe who work in the fields on vegetables.

The enterprise has been successful partly because we are blessed with good early land, earlier than the rest of the country, and because of a good rotation of crops. Billy is now growing around 120 acres of brassicas (cauliflower and cabbage), potatoes and grain in a regular circulation around the fields. He does well, in most seasons, on cauliflower when frost is limited; less well on cabbage, a low-margin gambler's crop very dependent on harsh weather elsewhere; and early potatoes.

I watch Billy work on our farm. He does not attempt to achieve the high yields of grain which would be prevalent in eastern England. We are happy with two tons an acre on spring barley and three tons an acre on winter barley. He tells me that his father never owned a sprayer for chemicals – that would be suicidal for most farmers today. Every field is ploughed, and use of Roundup, the most common chemical weedkiller, is limited. We are appalled at the notion that Roundup can be sprayed on cereals just before they are harvested. It cannot be right. We do not believe in organic farming, however – the latest, ongoing craze; it is really a racket to con the housewife into buying more expensively from supermarkets, thereby increasing their margins.

Finally in our discussion we get around to the inevitable subject of the supermarkets – those big monopolistic monsters, as uncontrolled today as Rockefeller's Standard Oil was in 1930s America.

The quality of food is nothing like as good as in the past. There was no cold storage and vegetables and seasonal produce found their way fresh, via wholesale markets, into local shops. Nowadays vegetables are held in cold storage until demand requires transport to take them to packing houses and supermarket distribution centres, from where they are sent out again, probably two weeks old, on a road journey of several hundred miles. Worse still for fruit and tomatoes, they are available all year round, regardless of seasonality and taste.

*

The Land's End peninsula was so isolated from the rest of the country until the railways arrived in the 1850s that there was no option but to be wholly self-sufficient; it was subsistence farming of the kind that my wife Miloska encountered in the hills of Slovenia during the Second World War.

The eighteenth century agricultural revolution, the rotation of crops with turnips and arable crops in eastern England, and the earlier enclosure movement hardly penetrated Cornwall. The small farms were already enclosed by granite hedges.

In the far west the fertility of the soil was maintained with dung, seaweed spread on the fields and calorific sand which was readily available from nearby dunes. There was an understanding of the importance of fallow and green manuring, and of clover in the pastures. The dramas caused by fluctuating commodity prices for grain, leading to the Corn Laws in 1818 until their repeal in 1846, were probably less severe in Cornwall, where the trading of agricultural produce was more restricted. Weather, floods and drought were the enemies of the harvest, as they still are today.

Going further back, we are fortunate to have the accounts of Trewinnard Farm in 1780. In some sense our farm was unusual because in those days it was owned by the Hawkins family, who derived their income from mining and from mortgages over declining estates like Godolphin, owned then by the Duke of Leeds. Trewinnard Farm covered around 100 acres then, but it had ten employees, paid a few pence each week.

The reason I have included farming in this book is not because we farm ourselves but because of the drastic social changes that we have seen over the past forty years or so since 1965. When we came to Cornwall – I as a carpet-bagger seeking a seat in Parliament – the county was dominated politically and socially by small farmers.

The changes have been dramatic. To give one example at the outset, in the small parish of Towednack on the moors near Land's End there were fifteen farms milking cows. Now there is one. Generally in the mid-sixties the average farmer was milking fifty cows on forty to sixty acres. The farmers were surviving because of the support the post-war Labour and Conservative governments gave to agriculture, but their time was nearly up.

Since those days there has been a huge consolidation of farm holdings, and I can now count only one or two in the district which struggle on, milking around 120 cows. Whereas most of the farms were employing one full-time man and often one part-timer in the 1960s, now none employ outside labour. Survival is dependent on grandfather, wife and elder son, all combining to work the farm, foregoing outside labour.

Our immediate neighbour, with his brother, is milking up to 400 cows a day on around 1,000 acres. As the small farmers have been forced out of business, so there has been an amalgamation of holdings – the consolidation mentioned above – to create larger farms, possibly more efficient so that they can afford the massive cost of farm machinery and modern milking parlours. We are going the way of New Zealand, where I have seen milking parlours catering for 1,000 cows a day.

I talked one day to another neighbour whose grandfather was killed in a threshing accident; his father started with a few acres and built a local transport business collecting farm animals for market, today run by his son. Most of the local markets, which were the weekly meeting place of the farmers for company and gossip, have been closed. This farmer/transport operator owns 600 acres, having started with virtually nothing, and runs a very large beef lot with two to three thousand cattle. All the cattle are collected from the remaining markets for store cattle in Exeter,

Truro and Tavistock, fed on straw and maize silage; and then transported to Lancashire, a mere 400 miles away, for slaughter.

Several things have caused the destruction of traditional small family farming in the West Country. The most pernicious influence has been the greed and monopoly of the supermarkets. Of course, Sainsbury's, Tesco and the like superficially compete with one another, but they follow and fix their prices in de facto collusion. Whatever the process, the impact is to undermine the stability of their suppliers in every field.

This has been made possible by two factors. First, the unwillingness of governments to control this behaviour by putting teeth into voluntary agreements between producers and supplier; second, but more important, has been the impact of globalization. It is possible for the supermarkets to dictate terms because they can always order their products from overseas. Of course, it suits government to see food prices forced down for the consumer – and to ignore the stability of the British food industry generally. Dependence on Europe for food imports and the export of farm produce have grown enormously.

Most farmers now have to run faster to stand still; they would say that however much they produce they can never improve their margins and make investment in modernization more possible. It is impossible to make a stand against the power of the supermarkets. Another factor is the bureaucracy forced on farms by the European Union. The young quite like the idea of farming, but are unprepared to knuckle down to the paperwork and form-filling which can take up to 50 per cent of a farmer's time. Why work seven days a week with all the stress that accompanies animal welfare when to obtain vital subsidy from the EU it is necessary to sit up half the night on a computer?

Because of the disappearance of so many farmers, Cornwall has changed away from agriculture, from mining and fishing into tourism, which now overwhelms the economy of the country.

In 1965 when we arrived on the scene, the Cornwall County Council was dominated by the farming community. The chairman was a landowner and probably two-thirds of the members who stood as Independents were in farming or its associated activities. The Independents controlled the Council in the 1970s and 1980s. Slowly politics wormed its way into

Council membership – and at the last election only four farmers were elected to the Council.

Socially, the farming community were everywhere in the sixties and seventies – that community has all but disappeared. In former days, the pubs were full of farmers and farm workers – and farming was a principal topic of conversation and gossip. Not now.

Interestingly, in the 1980s my wife ran a daffodil enterprise over seventy acres on our farm. Each day during the early spring season we employed up to seventy flower pickers. On piecework they could earn good wages. All of the flower pickers were from local families. Today it is not possible to recruit local families into agricultural work; virtually all the workers are from Eastern Europe. We cannot blame local families for finding more congenial work when it is available, but we cannot rule out the impact of the benefits system which can provide a more comfortable existence than backbreaking work in the rain and cold.

I got together with Billy Collins to discuss all this. I am a huge admirer of what he has achieved, against the odds. He did not dissent from the description that I have given in the early part of this chapter; his own family experience is interesting.

I do not attempt a conclusion. As both Billy and I acknowledge, the world moves on. Globalization has driven down prices. We cannot dis-invent the computer or nuclear weapons. Man's inventiveness and curiosity has created a more prosperous world. I have no nostalgia for the past, but it is interesting to remember how things were done – and how so many fell by the wayside while others grabbed the opportunity to make progress for themselves.

Chapter Thirteen

Miloska

Lady Nott

My wife Miloska has had the most extraordinary life. Perhaps my acquaintance with her cannot really be described as an 'encounter' since we have been married for nearly sixty years. When we met and married at Cambridge, those who knew us both gave the marriage a few months at best. How wrong they were.

Some of this chapter I have given over to Miloska's own words. When I wrote my memoir, *Here Today, Gone Tomorrow*, in 2002 I asked her to dictate memories of her early youth and later episodes. I include in this sketch extracts of what she told me at that time.

But first let me introduce her.

I have met few people who have had such a varied and sometimes tumultuous life. Miloska's is the story of the twentieth century: Austro-Hungary, war, Nazism, Communism, Catholicism, post-war Germany, Cambridge, the Bosnian War. She is a survivor.

Miloska was born in Maribor, the second city of Slovenia, then part of Yugoslavia, a town near the Austrian border, in 1935. The Germans called it Marburg an der Drau and made it part of Hitler's Third Reich. She hates the German name. Maribor is an industrial town, but it is attractive nonetheless, with Austro-Hungarian architecture and fine buildings alongside the River Drava.

Now I go over to Miloska's story. These are her own words:

> I was born in Maribor . . . about ten miles from the Austrian border. We were very much part of the old Austro-Hungarian Empire. There was a family problem, so I really grew up with my father. But just before the Nazis invaded I was put on a farm for protection, so that the Germans didn't connect me with my

father, who didn't know if it was safe with the Germans or not. He would come and collect me, and we would spend weekends together.

I loved the farm. I was freer, I could run about; they didn't dress me up in stiff collars and things. I have nothing but very happy memories of it. The family had four boys, who were all older than me, and one daughter. We were completely self-sufficient there – the only things we had to buy were coffee and sugar. They killed all their own pigs and cattle and preserved meat for the winter in pigs' fat. They had a small vineyard and made their own *slivovitz*. I still remember all the ways that we fed ourselves – I could survive today if we ever had to go back to subsistence agriculture; but I don't know how the urban population of this country, which has lost its knowledge of basic farming skills, would ever survive. When war broke out, the Germans came to the farm quite often, although there were no roads up to it. My hairstyle had to be changed because I had a fringe, and that would have shown that I was not a farmer's daughter. So I had to have two plaits, to make it appear that I was their daughter. I think the boys started to believe that I was really their sister. Every day I walked to the village school, which was several miles there and back, and in the winter there was a lot of snow. Slovenia is very cold in the winter.

My father's family had plenty of land and they had a good deal of businesses. My grandfather had made a lot of money – he had provided the grain and fed all the horses for the Royal Yugoslav Army. My father loved music, and he didn't really work for his living. He had a hotel in Maribor, and the Gestapo and SS would come to eat in its restaurant. And so the waitresses always knew who was due to be deported – they apparently had a tunnel under an old cemetery, and so people were smuggled away. As well as my father, there was a professor and some other people who dug this tunnel. They would hide the people who were intended to be deported to concentration camps for three or four days in this tunnel – and when the Germans stopped looking for these people, then they would get them up to the Pohorje Mountains, and they were safe because you couldn't find anybody at all in the mountains. So this went on until around 1944, and then the professor was caught, and apparently he was tortured and mutilated by the Gestapo, and people then say he gave my father away. I don't know exactly what happened when my father was taken to Dachau in 1944 – nearly at the end of the war.

In Dachau people had seen him. But they had so many stories. Some say that when the Americans bombed Dachau he was running with some other people over a bridge and this bridge was bombed. Then the other story, which is persisting still, is that he survived and that he came as far as the border and then the Communist partisans killed him. They killed many people who came from the old 'capitalist' families in Slovenia and they killed a lot of people returning from concentration camps because they did not understand how they had survived the Germans. But we have no proof, we don't know where he died, and there are many stories.

After the war I finished elementary school and wanted to go to further education. So I walked to Maribor by myself – it was about ten miles from the farm. I was nearly ten years old; the Nazis had gone and the Communists had taken over. I had no family to go to – my father was dead – so I was taken to a privileged sort of students' home where some of the children were orphans and others were children of famous heroes of the resistance to the Nazis. It was run by the Communist Party.

At this school I was brainwashed completely into Communism. I was made into the most enthusiastic eleven-year-old Communist that you could find. I presented a bouquet to Tito when he visited Maribor – funnily enough, Tito was a distant relation of my family.

Our patron at the school was the Red Star Army, the Yugoslav Army. We got everything from them. We were very privileged. It was rather like a Communist Eton in a way, and I was very happy there. We had a political afternoon, but basically our education was the same as anybody else's. Once at New Year – we didn't have Christmas ourselves, because we were Communists – we had to recite partisan poems in the officers' house, and the interesting thing was the heroes were always Serbs.

I had switched off from my own background. I wanted to be either a peasant's daughter or a hero's daughter; one thing I did not want to be was from the type of family that I came from, because that was shame. We had in this school a big picture of a fat, fat capitalist with a boy who was begging for food, and this capitalist takes a whip and he's going to hit him but not give him the bread. Every capitalist was bad; there were no good capitalists. Everything in the Western world was exploitation. One per cent of the population was very rich, that's how we were taught, the rest were all poor and starving. Of course, I believed every single word they said. You were not really a private person; you were the child of your country, and they were preparing you for your country.

I had never known my mother because of the family dispute. Eventually I found a relative of hers who said that she remarried in '43 – that she went to Split and was an interpreter because she spoke a lot of languages, and that then she married this chap from Rome and had gone to Italy.

I had not seen my mother since I was two months old, so it was quite difficult. I wrote to her and I got a very strange letter back. And I then remembered that I needed a passport. Somebody told me that a friend of my father was now Minister of Culture in Tito's government, I think, and he would see me. By this time I was sixteen and a half. He gave me a passport. He organized a passport for two weeks during my school holidays.

So then I wrote to my mother and said I'm coming. She said she would wait for me in Milan at the station, which she did. We went home and my mother just went out. The maid looked after me and my stepfather was kind to me, but she was never there. I was there two months and I wanted to escape.

I did escape – I escaped to the Yugoslav consul in Milan and he brought me back because I was a minor and then I escaped again three days later. But I remember that the Italian consul in Zagreb had said something funny – he must have known that my mother didn't really want me to come. The Italian consul had said, 'I want you to take this address. It was the famous Visconti family. If you have any problems, ring.' I rang this person, who said, 'Come to Como, and somebody will be waiting for you.' This was a princess from Naples, an old lady from an Italian royal family, and she talked to my mother and said, 'This girl will go back to Communism if you are not interested in her.' That was the last time I saw my mother.

The Italian princess became my guardian; she was very religious and, as a passionate Catholic, she wanted to save me from Communism. From that time on I never wanted for money or anything. She arranged for me to attend a convent school in Milan. I had a private tutor for the Italian language. I started at university. I wanted to take Russian again, but I had already done Russian for seven years, so she organized the Italian ambassador in Germany to arrange that I go to the Goethe Institute.

What I have not mentioned yet is that I had a terrible problem. When I came to Italy, I was looking for all these poor people and I couldn't find any, and I realized that everything I was told by the Communists was a lie. And now I couldn't understand how these people that I had trusted so much, who were more than my parents, who were everything to me over all those years – how they could lie so much? Also, some nuns in the convent school were not much different from the Communists; although they were good to me they were also trying to brainwash me. There was a priest who was continuously telling me that I should talk on the radio against the Communists. But I had this fear of the Communists and what they could do to me, even outside Yugoslavia. I wouldn't talk against Communism. Anyhow, I felt the nuns were similar to the Communists – they were both trying to ruin me.

When I first met Miloska in Cambridge she was under pressure from the Yugoslav Embassy and its spies. She was offered many invitations to attend dances in London, all of which she refused. I remember her telling me that she was riding her bicycle down the street when she was knocked down deliberately by a car. She reported it, and in due course Special Branch showed her a portfolio of photographs of agents at the Yugoslav Embassy. She identified three men immediately, two of them Serbs. Of course, the Communists in the late 1950s were not going to give up on her easily. She was an attractive, well-educated girl, brought up in a special Communist school, speaking several European languages. After that incident, I suspect, they backed away.

When I was Economic Secretary at the Treasury in the Heath government, my private secretary said that a gentleman from the Security Services wanted to interview me, a routine process, so I was told. He was a creepy little man, with a facial tick. My wife's past was never questioned, but I told him that we had a Yugoslav au pair. I refused to dismiss her but gave him her name, address and family connections. That was the last I heard from the Security Services, although I would be astonished if they failed to keep track of us both thereafter.

The truth must be told. When I was dealing later with security issues in government I developed the highest respect and admiration for counter-intelligence and MI5. But I have never been able to get my head around our 'spies'. It is a tricky task, spying on foreign countries, and several of my friends at university joined the Service as foreign agents. But I regarded any kind of spying, even spying for our country with some distaste – that is very unpatriotic of me.

I suppose it is appropriate – or perhaps inappropriate, given that I have been married so long – to record that I only met my wife three or four times before our marriage. For me, it was an immediate impulse; I had no control over my behaviour.

I hand over to my wife again:

> I had to go to the Cambridge Union. I can't remember what the debate was about, but John made a really very funny speech. Then I didn't see him for a while, until suddenly out of the blue I got an invitation to a tea party in John Nott's rooms. One of my fellow students at the language school was called Loretta, so she and I came to tea. I think there was another girl and two men called Julian Grenfell and Mark Roper – boys, really, and John was making tea, I remember that. Then the men started to

talk about shooting – about pigeon shooting. The whole thing for us was so unbelievably boring because we didn't know where they shot, what they shot, who shot well, who shot badly and who the people were. I think Loretta was more upset than me. I thought what boring people. Funny really, because Loretta married Julian and I married John!

Soon afterwards my fiancé and I thought it would be very nice if we had another engagement party, this time at Cambridge. So we organized it, and when I saw the invitation list I saw John Nott on it. I really went for my fiancé and I said, 'Why do you ask John? We don't need to ask him.' I think I felt a bit of danger. If I had felt immune it would have been perfectly all right. Anyhow, my fiancé was determined to have him. So we organized a party, and John did turn up, and I tried to completely ignore him; there were many people, but I didn't succeed because he approached me and said 'Hello' very cheerfully. And somehow, I don't know what happened, but he was then leaning against the entrance to the room and we started to talk. It was very embarrassing and my behaviour was really very bad. To tell you how nice my fiancé was, he never reprimanded me; but if I were my fiancé, I would have said, 'Look this was our engagement party and you spent half an hour talking to John Nott.' I can't remember what we were talking about much. All I remember is that he said, 'I love you and I'm going to marry you', and then he went. My party was finished – I couldn't concentrate on anything and all the time I was so angry. I was angry at him. How can he love me when this was only the third time he'd met me? And I just didn't enjoy it any more. I went home and I wrote in my diary, 'What a cheek, what a conceit, what a presumptuous male.'

Fair comment!

We were married in 1959. My last term at Trinity was rather testing. I was President of the Union, just married and, worst of all, I had done no work at all. For three years I never attended a lecture. The only task was to prepare one essay a week for a Law Professor called Mr Jolowitz.

There were three of us in the tutorial; the other two became Law Lords. Not me! There was no time or money for a honeymoon, so we went to a ghastly boarding house in Shaldon, South Devon; my new wife went out every day to chat to the fishermen. I struggled with the Law of Real Property. Ghastly, tedious rubbish. I got a second-class degree, a triumph in the circumstances.

Life went on. I started work in the City at Warburgs (see Chapter Two). We bought a terraced house in Islington in 1961 for £3,500. We had three children and they went to the best schools. Money was a problem, especially when I entered politics in 1966. But in those days newcomers to the Tory benches were only respected if they had sound military or business background and interests outside Parliament. Based on my City reputation I was able to earn a substantial income outside Parliament which financed the school fees and the purchase of a farm in Cornwall (see Billy Collins, Chapter Twelve). I cannot imagine anything worse than a full-time politician. I fear that Cameron and Osborne went straight into politics from the Conservative Research Department. I had won the parliamentary seat of St Ives in Cornwall, consisting of the Land's End and Lizard peninsulas and the Isles of Scilly, entirely due to the canvassing skills, charm and energy of my wife. I was tolerated in the constituency; she was loved by everyone who met her.

I suppose it must have been twenty years into our marriage that we were invited one day to the Yugoslav Embassy for dinner. I had been a junior minister in the Treasury and my political reputation was established. At dinner Miloska met the Yugoslav Counsellor, who had been a boy in Maribor and knew a lot about her family. As one Slovene to another he persuaded her to return to Yugoslavia and investigate her family background – I had never discussed her wartime experiences. She had shut her mind to her past; I respected her privacy and never enquired about it.

It turned out that my wife's story as she told it above is something of a sanitized version of her time in Nazi-occupied Yugoslavia. Although she was happy on her little farm, she never saw her father again. The Gestapo had a base in her local village, Sveti Jakob. When they patrolled the surrounding farms to hunt down deserters from the German army she was hidden in the cellar under a pile of turnips. Everyone lived a life of terror. The children were made to parade in the village to watch the execution of deserters.

Later, when she lived in Italy, she was sent by her guardian, the Italian princess, to Germany to learn the language. This is what she said:

> After leaving the convent I had a very intense course at the Goethe Institute. Then I went to an interpreters' school in Munich, where I was for nearly three years and I passed my exams there. I found it very difficult in Germany, because I could still remember the people who had died and the people who had been taken away. I remembered how on the farm next door to ours, the Germans took all the animals out and killed them, because the farm had clandestinely killed their pig and you had to have permission to kill a pig. Of course all the villagers talked about the people who had vanished under fascism. So it was difficult, and I have to say that, although I speak German reasonably well, I don't like the German language.
>
> Two incidents happened to me in Germany that I remember well. One is that I had a lecturer who had lost an arm in the war and he was continually saying, 'If we didn't do this or that, we would have won the war.' I hated him really, just for that. The other thing, which was so characteristic of the Germans, is this. We were all worked up about what was happening in Hungary, and we had a meeting of students from all around. There was a young German student, probably about twenty-five, and he was speaking and there wasn't a murmur. If a pin had dropped you would have heard it. And this sort of impressed me. And I think if he had said, 'Let's march now,' everybody would have followed him. Another thing that struck me in Germany was young mothers beating their children excessively – I had come from Italy and we don't beat our children. And then there was *Oktoberfest* – I have never, ever seen so much vulgarity. And people were so drunk and they were manhandling you. I never did go again.

So there are certain German characteristics which I dislike. I can't generalise that every German is like that, but I also had

a separate resentment because they had occupied my country.
So it was difficult . . .

In 1979 the Conservatives won the General Election and I became
successively Trade and then Defence Secretary. I travelled around the
world with my wife in an RAF VC10 aircraft. Margaret Thatcher, always
a fan of Miloska's, inspired a great deal of jealousy among ministers'
wives because she permitted Miloska alone to travel with her husband –
her language ability being the excuse. But it was resented by the other
senior ministers, whose wives had to stay at home!

After the Falklands War in 1983 I retired from politics. There had
been a deal. I had agreed with my wife, who disliked the idea of politics,
that I would leave it for business after fifteen years. I kept to the bargain.
Thereafter, Margaret Thatcher behaved towards me like a deserted wife:
her senior ministers did not abandon her in what she saw as a casual way.

Then began the next phase of Miloska's extraordinary life. She became
a farmer. The farm in Cornwall was losing money and needed hands-on
attention, so she decided to take control. She moved to Cornwall and for
the next twenty years I commuted on the night sleeper from Paddington
to Penzance, spending my weekends in the country.

Miloska continues:

> As only part of the land was used for bulbs and vegetables, which
> we had to circulate around the fields, we decided to buy some
> cattle. We chose pedigree Herefords with the idea of providing
> young bulls to the local dairy farmers. They were based on the
> Merryhill herd in Herefordshire, which had won the Burke
> Trophy at the Royal Show for its females; so we bought a bull
> called Merryhill Upstart and four cows. So while we were doing
> the daffodils we also started with a few Herefords.
>
> I was looking after these four cows which were in calf, and it
> was interesting because I had never in my life farmed. I grew
> up during the war on a little farm in Slovenia, and it's very
> interesting because the instinct of those five years as a child on
> the farm were still there, and of course the people, my family,
> always had land although they didn't work on the land. So it

wasn't something completely new to me to live out on the farm. We built up our herd to nearly a hundred head, and that was quite hard work because I found myself very often completely alone with the calving. In the early years there was a problem with a calf and I had to tie calving ropes on this calf's legs. I put myself on my tummy and I pulled the calf out like that, and the calf was alive, and I think that is the first time when I felt this amazing exultation about being able to calve any animal safely. And that is something that nobody will ever understand unless they have done it. I always think of Anna Karenina when Levin came back from St Petersburg very disappointed about love, and when he went back to his estate and the servants came out with a cloak and said, 'Daisy's had a calf', Levin forgot completely about his love affair in St Petersburg society, because this was his prize cow and she had a calf and it was safe. I must have read Anna Karenina in different languages at least three or four times, but I did not really understand it until I started to farm.

With the Herefords we just about broke even, but the problem with Trewinnard was that the land was too rich for Herefords and the bulls lost their size and got rather fat, so we were all the time losing the scale of the bull calves. But we did sell thirty or forty bulls for putting on the Friesian dairy cows – my progeny are well established in West Cornwall!

There were some incidents that were quite terrifying. Because our grass was very luscious we had a great problem with magnesium deficiency, which is called staggers, in spite of the fact that we pumped magnesium into the cows in the spring. One year we lost three valuable pedigree cows and the vet could not come in time, so John and I had to learn how to stab the cow to let out the gases from its stomach. The vet showed me the area, but of course it is the most difficult thing to do because the cow's skin is so hard. There was me stabbing and stabbing and unless I succeeded the cow was going to die. Anyhow eventually I managed to stab correctly and all these terrible gases came out. It's really quite revolting. Then the cow got up and fell down, and then got up again and fell down, because they suffer shock.

I really thought I would lose the cow, but in fact it survived. I have never had an experience of doing something like that. It took another ten years off my life.

*

Now to later history.

In 1990 the Serbian-led Yugoslav army, always thirsting after a 'Greater Serbia', invaded Bosnia. The Yugoslav army had earlier tried to close the Slovene border with Austria, near my wife's wartime home. It was fought off by locally led Slovene volunteers. After Tito died, the Slovenes and Croats, who generated the wealth of Yugoslavia, were never going to accept second-class citizenship under the Serbs. The attitude of the Croats and Slovenes to Serbia was crudely expressed at the time of the creation of Yugoslavia in 1918 by the Croat leader at the Paris Peace Conference when he said, 'You are not going to compare, I hope, the Croats, the Slovenes and the Dalmatians, who have centuries of artistic, moral and intellectual communion with Italy, Austria and Hungary, with these half-civilised Serbs, the Balkan hybrids of Slavs and Turks!'

Slovenia voted 92 per cent to abandon Yugoslavia. The British government, under John Major and Douglas Hurd, tried to frustrate Slovene independence from Communist Yugoslavia, a typical act of Foreign Office stupidity at a time when we were encouraging other countries to break free of Communism.

I had wanted my wife to dictate her experiences in the Bosnian War in her own words, but she declined. The whole crisis was too recent and distressing for her, so I am recording what she told me.

She said that only someone who had lived through the terrible experiences of the Second World War could understand the fear that war and occupation generate, especially among children.

When the Yugoslav army abandoned Slovenia it went on to slaughter hundreds of Croats in Vukovar. Then the BBC started reporting how 36,000 Muslim refugees had fled the invasion of Bosnia, escaping mass murder and rape. My wife went to Slovenia to investigate and with the Slovene Red Cross she helped the refugees in hastily erected camps. She spoke their language and realized that she had to help.

On returning to England she contacted the Foreign Office to explain what was happening in Bosnia, but the Foreign Secretary could not see her for several weeks, so she went to Margaret Thatcher. Margaret said that she must establish a charity – the Fund for Refugees in Slovenia – and she agreed to be patron and made the first personal donation, of £10,000. Miloska's charity went on to raise £4 million in money and goods to help the victims of the Bosnian War.

My wife appeared on British television to describe her experiences and made a broadcast on Radio Cornwall. The second donation came from our eighty-four-year-old neighbour on the adjoining farm; she pulled on her gumboots and crossed the fields to give her week's pension to the charity.

My wife then organized food from two food companies, Hillsdown and Heinz, and clothing from Women's Institutes which was taken to the refugees in Slovenia by nine lorries provided freely by the Royal Mail. Schools were established in the camps, where many of the refugees were teachers.

As the war in Bosnia created more refugees, there was a desperate need for medicine and medical equipment in Tuzla hospital in eastern Bosnia which was surrounded by Serb forces and their irregulars. The hospital sent a doctor and two lorries to collect the medicine which Miloska had organized with Glaxo. For one whole week the Herzegovinians, the Bosnian Croats, held up the lorries in an attempt to purloin the medicines on board, but she stuck with it.

Fortunately, we knew the Croatian Ambassador in London, and through him the government in Zagreb demanded the opening of the border to let the lorries pass. With large pictures of pigs on the side of the lorries to show that the supplies could not be for Muslims, Miloska crossed the mountains under shellfire and in constant danger, but the medicines got through to Tuzla hospital.

The EU was divided, as always in a crisis, and hopelessly incompetent, so eventually peace was brokered by the Americans – after the siege of Sarajevo, endless atrocities by the Serb army and its murderous irregulars, and the infamous slaughter of 8,000 Muslim men and boys in Srebrenica.

Miloska spent seven years in and out of Srebrenica and supervised personally the building of 150 houses for the victims, mainly the surviving women and children, of the massacre, as well as medical centres and schools in the area.

It is important to record that 90 per cent of the £4 million raised by her charity came from Jewish individuals and charities; only Jewish people understood the nature of a holocaust, albeit one of innocent Muslims. I salute my wife: her triumph was one of organization and perseverance. In 2012 she was awarded an OBE for her work.

Chapter Fourteen

Margaret Thatcher

Prime Minister

Unlike Geoffrey Howe, Nigel Lawson and Norman Tebbit, I was not a major player in the long years of the Thatcher government. But I had an important ringside seat in the first Thatcher government, which was the most difficult and controversial period of her long reign.

As Trade Secretary I abolished the Prices and Incomes Policy, announced the first privatization of the new government, British Airways, and was a dedicated advocate of abolishing exchange control. I became one of her most trusted Cabinet supporters, serving on her two key Cabinet committees, the Economic Committee and the Overseas and Defence Policy Committee.

She rewarded me with the post of Defence Secretary in 1981: it was more difficult thereafter, but we always had a friendly if testing relationship.

I am so glad that I resigned my post and left politics in 1983, because my loyalty would have been severely tested in her later years. Had I held a senior post, which I am sure that I would have done, in the final drama I fear that I would have advised Margaret to step down. It is fatal for any Prime Minister to serve more than ten years. Hubris inevitably sets in.

My relationship with her went back several years before she became Prime Minister. Ted Heath asked me to be her deputy in Opposition after we had lost the election in 1974. I had hated my time in the Treasury during the so-called Barber boom and I thought that Ted Heath's days were numbered. In his graceless way, sitting in a chair drinking whisky, he asked me to remain in his team under Shadow Environment Secretary Margaret Thatcher. I discussed it with her but declined the offer because I wanted to be free, morally, to kick Ted Heath out. It happened, and I was an enthusiastic supporter of Margaret Thatcher's candidacy.

Before that time I was a financial adviser to Burmah Oil, where Denis Thatcher was a director. He and I had several discussions about Margaret's future, and I think that I was one of the earliest proposers that she should stand for the leadership.

'What a ghastly idea,' said Denis. 'I trust that will never happen.'

I encountered her also two years running, after she became leader, on the moors in Islay, the Scottish preserve of the Morrison family, who were major power brokers in the Tory Party. Peter Morrison had developed a club which called itself 'Toffs for Margaret'. I was never a toff, but he invited me to stay with his father, John Morrison, Lord Margadale, at the Morrison *schloss* in Islay. Peter's idea was that I, as a coming star in the Tory Party, would sit up late with Margaret discussing politics. After stalking all day, I retired to bed after dinner exhausted and Margaret was bereft. It is surprising that this behaviour did not wreck my future political career.

However, while Denis escaped to play golf each day, my wife Miloska developed a friendship with Margaret, who came on picnics dressed in clothes more suitable to an evening event in Finchley. She was charming in Scotland but entirely out of place, not being a hunting, shooting and fishing type dressed in tweeds. My wife's friendship was refreshed with vigour when Margaret became violently antagonistic towards John Major and Douglas Hurd over their handling of the Bosnian crisis. She became the patron of and contributor to my wife's charity in favour of the Bosnians who had fled the massacre in Srebrenica.

I joined the Shadow Cabinet shortly after Margaret had been elected as leader. Being essentially cautious and uncertain by nature, she appointed a raft of Heath's former ministers to the Shadow Cabinet, including people like Reggie Maudling. Few of them wished her well. The atmosphere was poisonous. She did her best to hold her new team together, but they ganged up against her in argument. I recall that the most cynical, supercilious member was Chris Patten, who was head of the Conservative Research Department – the members of that Department referred to her as 'Hilda'. Patten sat at the end of the table smirking and grinning as the Heath brigade tried to cut her down in argument. Oxford University and the BBC deserved this 'pooh-bah' of a man, a classical representative of liberal metropolitan England, which marvellously, if belatedly, saw its Armageddon in the EU Referendum. I think her experience of the Shadow Cabinet convinced her that she had no choice but to be a fighter, with a contempt for the political establishment that she inherited. She felt uncomfortable with the condescension and entitlement of the Eton brigade – Gilmour, Pym, Carrington, Soames – who were over-represented in the Cabinet. In her memoir she recalled that when she had a stormy meeting with Christopher Soames to sack him from the Cabinet, she 'got the distinct impression that he felt the natural order of things was being violated and that he was, in effect, being dismissed by his housemaid'.

In her early days she did not triumph in Parliament as Leader of the Opposition, possibly the worst job in the country. Opponents on the back benches like Julian Critchley, a friend of Michael Heseltine, suggested that colleagues should write to her as 'Leader of the Opposition, c/o Dickens & Jones'. Such snobbery! But slowly, by kindness and appreciation, she built up a following on the Tory back benches, never failing to charm them. The constituency party – in those days large – loved her, and she was good at set speeches to her natural middle-class supporters.

Anyone writing a history of the Tory Party in recent times will record the time and effort that Margaret Thatcher undertook to keep the constituency parties happy. She made endless visits around the country encouraging constituency workers in their support for the Party in Parliament. She avoided centralizing control of the Party in Central Office. She would never have created special lists of candidates in the same image as the members of the metropolitan elite from Oxbridge, Central Office and public schools.

In Harold Macmillan's day the Party in the country numbered 2.4 million – but slid as a result of pure neglect and arrogant disdain to around 100,000 in David Cameron's. (Lessons can be learned from this. The Conservative Party will have a difficult time winning the next election if it cannot create a real locally controlled organization of enthusiastic younger people who believe in the Conservative mission. It is up against at least half a million enthusiastic Corbyn supporters who are on the doorstep every weekend. What does the Conservative Party offer today in response? An occasional gathering of elderly ladies at annual fêtes, and ubiquitous wine and cheese evenings.)

So to the early days in government. Margaret, more or less out of caution again, moved the Heath brigade into her first Cabinet, and they did their best to oppose the need for tough economic policies. She wisely bypassed the major doubters in the full Cabinet by moving power to selected members of the Economic Committee, of which I was one with Keith Joseph, Geoffrey Howe and John Biffen. We used to meet over breakfast at No. 10 to discuss the more difficult economic measures needed. But the quarrels with the full Cabinet continued. One of the worst aspects of the period was the leaking of the differences in the Cabinet to the press. I believe the worst offenders were Norman St John-Stevas, Leader of the House, and Ian Gilmour in the Foreign Office, both of whom she wisely dismissed in an early re-shuffle in 1981.

Margaret responded by gossiping to her friends about her difficulties, and the divisive concept of 'wets and drys' became the story. I thought it was disgraceful behaviour by her own supporters, who always succeeded in provoking a vicious article by a liberal journalist in the press. So tit for tat in the newspapers was the talk of the day. Margaret should have stopped it, but it was in her nature to fight back; she was a belligerent being. I referred to this practice in my farewell letter at the end of this chapter.

So the early days in government were vexing in the extreme. Recovery from 'The Winter of Discontent' of 1978–9 was slow. Unemployment, inflation and social discontent were all rising. Geoffrey Howe's budget in 1981 was a major turning point in the reputation of the government. It was exceptionally courageous, and it caused more bad publicity for the government than almost any other event in Thatcher's time in government. All personal allowances and tax thresholds were frozen. Extra taxes were imposed on alcohol and tobacco, cars and vehicle excise duty. The overall impact was to reduce the government's borrowing requirement from £14.5 billion to £10 billion. This was at a time when inflation was running at 13 per cent – and unemployment was rising to two million. If the budget was bold it was also politically very courageous.

The Cabinet was deeply antagonistic, but Margaret Thatcher forced it through. It led to the famous letter from more than 300 economists condemning the budget as a disaster. In fact, it was the turning point in the government's fortunes. Why do the economics forecasts always get it so wrong! I think she would have won the next election without the Falklands victory behind her – although the Falklands ensured it.

But the story does not end there.

This was at a time that riots were taking place in several cities. It is best described in Jonathan Aitken's outstanding biography of 2013:

> Speaking after a night of fresh rioting in Toxteth, Heseltine said that Howe's proposals would cause despair in the inner cities and bring electoral disaster for the government. He advocated a pay freeze. This would have been an astonishing U-turn. Nevertheless this heresy, striking at the root of everything that Margaret Thatcher stood for, was also supported by Peter Walker and Lord Soames. Worse was to come from the Lord Chancellor, Lord Hailsham, who spoke in doom-laden language about how in the 1930s unemployment had given birth to Herbert Hoover's Great Depression in the United States and Hitler's Nazi Party in Germany. Without making the same comparison, Jim Prior, Francis Pym and Ian Gilmour were almost as pessimistic about the government's strategy.
>
> With the temperature rising, Margaret Thatcher became 'extremely angry', particularly as some of her most trusted allies defected to the wets. She was astonished when John Biffen switched sides for the first time, saying that public spending should be allowed to rise. An ever worse betrayal in her eyes came from John Nott, who launched a withering attack on the Treasury's figures. 'All at once,' Margaret Thatcher recalled, 'the whole strategy was at issue. It was as if tempers suddenly broke.'
>
> These bitter divisions brought the government to the brink of a disastrous split. Feuds with the wets had been a festering sore for over two years, but suddenly they were winning by a clear and outspoken majority. Willie Whitelaw did his best to paper over the cracks with a loyal summing up. Yet even he, after rejecting the pay freeze, gave a warning against breaking the tolerance of society.
>
> Margaret Thatcher had to face the reality that only she and three of her 23 cabinet ministers, Geoffrey Howe, Keith Joseph

and Leon Brittan, the new Chief Secretary of the Treasury, fully supported her economic strategy. She closed the cabinet on a subdued note. She retired from the fray as a wounded Prime Minister. Her wounds hurt. The late summer of 1981 was the lowest point of her time in 10 Downing Street, apart from the dark days when she was ousted from power some 9 years later.

A memorandum sent to Margaret Thatcher at the zenith of her troubles in the autumn of 1981 was possibly the most brutal internal note ever sent to any Prime Minister; it came from members of her own No. 10 staff. It was clearly offensive and was headed 'Your political survival'. It was prepared by John Hoskyns, David Wolfson and Ronnie Millar, a theatre impresario and friend who wrote her speeches. A key sentence in the memorandum read: 'You break every rule of good man management. You bully your weaker colleagues. You criticise colleagues in front of each other and in front of their officials. They cannot answer back without appearing disrespectful in front of others to a woman and to a prime minister. You abuse that situation.'

She replied: 'I got your letter. No one has ever written a letter like that to a prime minister before.'

The statements were stark: 'You lack management competence. Your leadership style is wrong. The result is an unhappy ship. You have an absolute duty to change the way you operate.'

In fact the letter was true, but very unfair.

And then, out of the blue, came the Falklands crisis in 1982. I deal with it pretty fully in my chapter on Admiral Terry Lewin so I will not repeat it here. But the remarkable aspect of it was that Margaret Thatcher changed, with only the occasional lapse from her natural belligerence. I report one incident below. There was something about this, the greatest crisis in her long reign, and the calming presence of Terry Lewin, which changed her. She was a brilliant war leader. I saw her several times a day, and although she raged privately against Ronald Reagan and his urging of a negotiated settlement – or surrender as she would put it – she took all the key decisions methodically and bravely as we went along. She was particularly angry and often unreasonable with the appeasement urged by the Foreign Secretary, Francis Pym; but voices were never raised in the War Cabinet.

Many of the decisions were particularly difficult. There were concerned voices in the Ministry of Defence about the dangers of the landing in St Carlos Bay, without land-based air cover. She agreed to go ahead. The change to the Rules of Engagement – to allow the sinking of the *Belgrano* – actually caused no hesitation. The more vexing questions were whether to authorize the shooting down of South American civil aircraft which were spying on the sailing Task Force. This was not agreed. Many of the problems arose in the interface between the protection of the Task Force and the actions of outsiders, not least the Russian spy ships, rows with the BBC which behaved disgracefully throughout, and so on.

Although she did not show it to me, or publicly, her immediate entourage in No. 10 saw her personal crisis over the sinking of the *Sheffield*, *Coventry* and others of our ships. I find it interesting only because I do not think that she ever allowed herself to ponder independently the full nature of the risks that we were undertaking. She made up her mind to recapture the Falklands – and did not consider the risks in a way that any man might have done. In my memoir I declared the triumph as a 'woman's war'. Most of us assumed that we would lose many ships and men and, when losses happened halfway through the conflict, most of us were saddened but it did not come as a surprise or shock. It shocked Margaret Thatcher. She was certainly aggressive and belligerent by nature but she was never warlike. Although it is not her reputation, she was a naturally kind person.

So I add one 'incident' when her impatience with any appeasement spilled over; the strain was showing and it is understandable. It occurred about halfway through the negotiating process. Again I resort to Aitken's biography to describe it:

> With military moves so far advanced, and the landing on the Falklands planned for 21 May (almost the last possible date for weather reasons), the Prime Minister grew increasingly irritated with those who kept urging her to make further diplomatic concessions. President Reagan was not the only one to catch the rough edge of her tongue on this issue. At a meeting of the

war cabinet at Chequers on 17 May, she was bitterly sharp with Francis Pym and his team of senior Foreign Office diplomats who were drafting a final ultimatum to Argentina.

The unpleasant wrangling at this meeting showed Margaret Thatcher at her most aggressive. At various moments she accused the five Foreign Office representatives, Sir Anthony Parsons, Sir Nicholas Henderson, Sir Michael Palliser, Sir Antony Acland and Francis Pym of 'being wet, ready to sell out, unsupportive of British interests' and lacking resolution. At one point she asked, 'Did the Foreign Office have no principles?' For good measure, she added the insult that while the Foreign Office 'were content to be dishonest and consult with dishonest people, she was honest'.

At this moment John Nott attacked her for being unfair. She counter-attacked, shouting him down for being rude! These rough tactics described by various participants as 'A totally horrendous bull session', or more loftily as 'Mrs Thatcher's High Noon with the FO', caused its most senior official to offer his resignation. 'At one moment when I thought she was being unnecessarily critical', recalled Antony Acland, 'I said, "If you want to get another Permanent Under-Secretary, for heaven's sake do".' After a long pause, the Prime Minister backed down. 'All right, no more Foreign Office bashing', she replied in a grudging tone.

Her behaviour was unacceptable because, to my surprise, these same Foreign Office officials had behaved extremely well throughout the drama, not least because the Foreign Secretary, Francis Pym, was obsessed with getting a negotiated settlement and his officials were suspended between their appeasing boss and a belligerent Prime Minister.

I hope that I have shown up the tensions and dramas of the first Thatcher government. After I had left politics it changed. Following her huge success in the 1983 election, and after the Falklands victory, her grip on the political scene became absolute. She became the great dragon-slayer and political heroine and she dominated the international scene. She and Reagan together fought and won the Cold War. She sacked without much protest the believers in the Macmillan and Heath consensus. The politics of decline, so well managed by the Civil Service, were given short shrift.

The most important feature of her time was her strength of personality – this was the force that drove her forward, crushing the obstacles in her path. She challenged the comfortable consensus of the status quo at every opportunity. She was a great Tory radical, despising Whiggish security and comfort. If she was always especially kind to her staff, she could be difficult with her Ministers and with those who did not share her vision of the way forward.

I believe her success became so evident after 1983 that she got quite grand – and from the uncertain and hesitant Prime Minister of my time her humility gave way to hubris. She became a heroine to the hard-worn peoples of Eastern Europe, an icon in the struggle by women against dominant men, she opened up the opportunities for tenants to become homeowners, and as the 1981 budget of Geoffrey Howe began to transform the UK economy, so the media adopted the messages that the Iron Lady of the Falklands was also the author of a new economic policy called Thatcherism.

There were two bleak incidents in her later years, both of which contributed to her downfall; both involved her Chancellors. Even in my time, she bullied Geoffrey Howe remorselessly. His slow, pondering, lawyer-like approach to issues irritated her and made her impatient with him. When he finally backed his successor Nigel Lawson in supporting the ERM and the shadowing of the deutschmark, her irritation with him spilled over. Nigel Lawson was an excellent Chancellor until he too fell for that ridiculous notion that a fixed exchange rate can help to bolster discipline in an economy. How such an intelligent man, now a rabid Brexiteer like me, can have supported the ERM astounds me. As the shadowing of the deutschmark generated a boom and rising inflation in the economy, Margaret Thatcher came to rely more on her economic adviser, Alan Walters. When Walters went round the City criticizing the policies of the Chancellor she should have sacked him; instead she forced Nigel Lawson into resignation. It was a classic example of a Prime Minister who had become too powerful and dominant. She was to go.

The manner of her going was catastrophic for the Conservative Party, and it has never really recovered from that event. The Tory Party decided after three General Election victories that she had become a loser – and surprisingly John Major won an election victory, which she could not have done. But it would have been better for the Conservative Party and the country if Thatcher had gone down at an election, not as a result of a rebellion by her Cabinet; it was born out of exhaustion with her inability to listen, and to her Ministers that seemed like overwhelming arrogance. The country had had enough of her and should have voted her out accordingly. There would have been no Blair and three decent but not especially interesting Prime Ministers, Major, Cameron and May.

It is hard to wrap this portrait up in a positive way because it ended badly. But Margaret, through the force of her personality, was a very great Prime Minister. She transformed the fortunes of the country, and for anyone to say that some other unknown man or woman could have achieved what she achieved is surely nonsense. She was unique.

I was accused by the press of writing her a private love letter when I left politics. It was no such thing. I found her irritating at times, but she loved an argument, did not take offence at disagreement and drove on however rough the seas ahead of her. My private letter which somehow became public read as follows:

My Dear Margaret,

I shall not be speaking in the Franks Debate but I wanted to send you this personal letter of support and encouragement . . . In my letter of resignation I said a number of things publicly about your Leadership, but public letters cannot say what I really feel about our friendship over fifteen years in Government and Opposition. Our friendship has been sustained for me through years of happy co-operation and occasional fierce disagreement (tinged with moments of positive dislike on both sides, I suspect) by your wonderful personality.

It is inexcusable to say so nowadays, but I actually admire you as a Woman! I think your instinctive approach to so many issues, so very unmasculine, is the secret of your success in the male-dominated world of politics.

Today there is no way that a consensus approach to the Nation's problems can overcome them. Until you gained the Leadership we were a Whips' Party. I am glad that we are now a gut-instinct Party . . . Given the immensity of your task and the support that you need to sustain your courage and conviction, it would be invidious of me to offer any caution, but I cannot restrain myself from one remark which you will not like. The Government will succeed or fail in the next six to seven years because the British people approve of it collectively. The personal loyalty and dedication of your Political Press Advisers in No. 10 I do not question, but the Lobby and the Corridors of Parliament are a dangerous place. I think it is utterly divisive and destructive to good Government if the Parliamentary Lobby-system is used to sustain the PM, or No. 10's views of life, against the Cabinet generally, or individual colleagues. You would never countenance such a thing I know, but it should not happen.

I do not mean to end on a sour, patronizing or critical note because that, I hope, is not the tenor of my final letter. I wish you God speed. You are doing a marvellous job in an almost impossible environment. Fortunately we are blessed by an outstanding Civil Service, for whom I have nothing but praise and admiration, albeit they need pushing and shoving now and again.

I wish you and Denis every personal happiness and success as the task continues.

Love
John

As my letter said, I disliked the way that Thatcher's cronies used the press to undermine her Ministers when they had a disagreement with her. It happened to me after my desertion of the Treasury at the famous meeting in 1981. But it was not the reason that I left politics in 1983, after the Falklands victory. I had promised my wife that I would return to business after fifteen years in politics, and I kept to that agreement.

My time in politics had its ups and downs, but I greatly enjoyed it; and I found my time in government particularly absorbing, especially when I made my greatest contribution to government as Secretary of State for Trade. It was no break to give up politics when I did.

I started my career as a regular soldier and ended it as Secretary of State for Defence – no one could ask for anything more from politics than that – and I owe much of it to Margaret Thatcher.

Chapter Fifteen

Douglas Shilcock

Prep school headmaster

Douglas Shilcock saved my life. He was headmaster for thirty-three years of a preparatory school called King's Mead, which had been evacuated to Devon from Seaford, in Sussex, at the beginning of the Second World War. I have nothing but praise for Douglas and his school, and in the light of this I must first touch on the vexed subject of bullying and abuse in the public school system which was established in Victorian times as a training ground of the future governors of the Empire.

When my father left for the war, as I said in my Introduction to this book, I was sent at the age of eight to a succession of really beastly schools. There was one particularly nasty one called The Grange at Honiton. The headmaster of The Grange was a sadistic bully and probably a homosexual, who took pleasure from regularly beating boys on their bare bottoms, the food was based on disgusting wartime rations and there was a complete absence of any care or affection. I was miserable.

Why my father should have wished a boarding school on his son at the age of eight is a mystery to me. All his life he used to talk about the horrible headmaster at a preparatory school called Cheam, which was attended by Prince Charles, two generations later. My father and his two younger brothers were at Cheam in the early 1920s and they evidently achieved some notoriety as Nott Major, Minor and Minimus. According to my father it was a cruel and unpleasant regime with regular beatings, but he survived it, with no long-term harm, as far as I am aware, except unhappy memories. Would-be parents who are thinking of sending their young sons to Cheam should alert Prince Charles for a recommendation.

The experiences of young boys sent to boarding school at eight years old are described in a book by Alex Renton published in 2017 called *Stiff*

Upper Lip. He has used all his journalistic flair to greatly exaggerate the trauma experienced by children at traditional private schools. By gathering anecdotal stories from grown-up people who suffered from bullying, abuse and gratuitous caning, he has painted a bleak picture of traditional English schooling. Hailed at the time as 'a brave and necessary book' and 'shocking, gripping and sobering', I thought it was awful, prostrating itself for liberal newspapers like the *Observer* and the *Guardian*.

Renton is the son of an excellent man who was a scholar at Eton and went on to become Chief Whip in Margaret Thatcher's administration. I knew him well. He was the last person to have disregarded the welfare of his son.

Traditional private education had many faults, which have largely been corrected, but, like so many journalists, Renton, in my opinion, let the side down for the sake of a 'story'. This practice is sometimes excused as 'investigative journalism'. I went from King's Mead to a public school called Bradfield. Bradfield was all about games and classical education. The headmaster in my day was Colonel Hills, a former housemaster and Commandant of the Eton Corps. He stalked around in Eton fancy dress, and we called him the 'overdressed waiter'. The dormitories were cold, the food quite terrible, fagging – junior boys carrying out minor chores for their seniors – was the order of the day and beatings by masters and senior boys not uncommon. It was awful really, but I survived it and I believe I was generally happy. Today, thanks to the introduction of girls into the sixth form, Bradfield has become one of the happiest and most civilized schools in the country.

When I wrote my memoir *Here Today, Gone Tomorrow* I said that the experience of my public school equipped me relatively well to face my first few weeks as a National Serviceman in the Army:

> The first six weeks in the army were traumatic for most young men but not for the public school boys, who were already inured to a life of humiliation, grilling, discipline and extreme discomfort. For the majority who had never left home and had been indulged by a loving mother, it was a dreadful change. Suddenly all those young men were thrown together, in rowdy dormitories with Brummies, Mancunians, Cockneys, Jocks, Geordies, Borstal

Trewinnard Farm from the air. St Michael's Mount top left, St Ives bay top right. Oil painting by Marcus May.

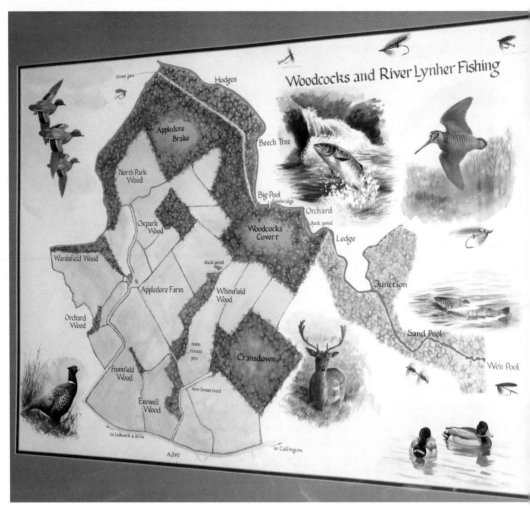

River Lynher fishing and sporting estate, Cornwall. Painted by Ashley Boon, 1988.

Presentation of the Sword of Honour to Anthony Fortescue, Coldstream Guards, in August 1982. The author had the great privilege of making the presentation on the recommendation of General Bramall, then Chief of the General Staff.

Left: Harvest at Trewinnard by Matthew Collins. An exciting time of the year.

Below: Western Area Ploughing Match. In spite of coaching by Billy Collins, the author always came bottom of the Novices Class.

The Cabinet in 1981. Front row from left: Peter Walker, Jim Prior, Keith Joseph, Peter Carrington, William Whitelaw, Margaret Thatcher, Quintin Hogg, Geoffrey Howe, Francis Pym, John Nott, Michael Heseltine. In the back row are: Norman Tebbit (2nd left), Norman Fowler (4th left), John Biffen (5th left), Leon Brittan (4th right), Nigel Lawson (3rd right) and Cecil Parkinson (2nd right).

Welcome to Cap Weinberger, US Secretary of Defense, 'our most important ally during the Falklands War'.

Above: Trewinnard – Hereford bull (Merryhill Upstart) and Dorset ewe, Woodcock and Mallard. Painted by Ashley Boon.

Below: From the author's game book.

Margaret Thatcher and Admiral Lewin at the Falklands Victory Parade, 1982.

boys, graduates and illiterates. The coarseness, vulgarity and language of the barrack room must have come as a real shock. Sex was the only unifying force – and was virtually the only topic of conversation!

Well, there you are, that's life – or life as it was. Was it better that a boy suffered a few days of homesickness at a boarding school at the age of eight – or the delayed shock of real life at the age of seventeen? It happens at some point in life, however cosseted a man may be.

After The Grange my life had changed dramatically. My mother discovered King's Mead School, which was located in a large manor house near Bideford in North Devon. Douglas Shilcock was, I think, one of the small contingent that greatly influenced my life for the better. He gave me self-confidence, a great blessing which has seen me through this life. I have pondered the subject of self-confidence among the young. How should it be encouraged? Self-confidence is different from superiority. I have gone through life observing what good schools offer to their children in this regard. And because my two sons, my forebears and my son-in-law all went to Eton, I take this school as an object lesson on this subject.

What is it that instils a sense of entitlement among Etonians? They all carry it around in varying degrees; a very few, only a very few, become arrogant. Is it the fancy dress, the pride in a hugely successful school, the camaraderie engendered by an almost military establishment? Etonians are certainly self-confident, but I don't like their sense of entitlement.

As this chapter is about education, I include a letter sent in February 1819 by my ancestor General Nott from Barrackpore, India, to his sons in Wales. I think it is a classic. Charles, the eldest, and William, the second son, were sent to school with a Mr Williams of Carmarthen. The letter reads as follows:

I hope I shall find that you have made great progress in learning. I should be sadly disappointed indeed were I to find it otherwise, as my best and fondest hope of happiness depend upon the knowledge of my boys.

I have requested your uncle to send you immediately to some public school, which will probably be Eton.

I am depriving myself of many comforts to enable me to see you well educated; but I shall feel myself amply, nobly repaid, if your conduct equals my fond expectation.

I trust you will be particularly careful in forming acquaintances while at Eton. Always bear in mind that virtuous poverty is far preferable to titled vice and indolence. Not that you may meet with those among the rich and great, who are possessed of every good and desirable quality; however, never lose sight of the old proverb – noscitur a sociis. It is not easy to get rid of evil companions where an intimacy has once subsisted with gay and dissolute young men. I would therefore have you be cautious in forming friendships. Never allow the supercilious smile of the idle and superficial, or the loud laugh of the ignorant, lead you, even for a moment, from the path of learning, honour, truth, and virtue; the pride of the supercilious is even beneath contempt. But though you will meet with many such characters, you will also find every good principle and disposition combined in others, whose acquaintance will confer honour, and whose friendship I would have you cultivate . . .

You must be great tall fellows by this time; your mother and myself anxiously look forward to the period of meeting. Farewell my much loved boys. Your mother joins in love to all. Write to me frequently, and tell of all you see and think.

Yours, affectionately,
William Nott
Barrackpore, Feb. 9 1819

At King's Mead, Douglas Shilcock loved his boys, cared for them physically and intellectually. The headmaster's dormitory adjoined his bedroom, and each morning the elite who occupied this dormitory used to pile into his room for conversation, ragging and the odd pillow fight.

I have exchanged several reminiscences about Douglas's dormitory with a number of my distinguished contemporaries. Today, of course, if it was known that we played games in his bedroom, he would be locked up in Pentonville as a sex abuser, and a great influence for good would have been lost to the world of education. The accusation which exists that he was a homosexual seems unfair when he was headmaster of this famous prep school for thirty-three years. How did he survive if this suggestion is correct?

In this controversial area, I was aware that, in the private school environment of the twentieth century, masters sometimes disappeared and did not return. Catholic schools had a steady turnover of arriving and departing priests. Monks and bishops hearing of alleged abuse did not go running to the police, but dealt with any problems privately. I think young boys generally knew how to look after themselves and were resistant to behaving like victims. A jealous boy who invented stories of abuse was dealt with swiftly. The whole 'abuse' obsession has got out of hand, instigated by a prurient press in today's ghastly emphasis on political correctness.

At Moreton, the manor house where we were located, we benefited greatly from Douglas's relationship with the booming wartime black market. He had stored large quantities of tinned food in the attic in case of an invasion. No one had heard of sell-by dates, a racket invented by the supermarkets. Our diet supplemented by fruit and vegetables from a large walled garden, we lived a life of considerable luxury. Douglas also seemed to have a unique access to women's silk stockings, impossible to obtain in wartime Britain; it made him hugely popular with women visitors, and a steady flow of mothers came to visit their sons. Douglas was charming to all of them, offering them vegetables from the walled garden and silk stockings if he liked the mother. The more aristocratic mothers, of which there were several, sometimes stayed in the adjoining cottage with Sir Hugh Stuckley, the owner of the Moreton estate.

Possibly the most interesting mother, certainly for me, was a famous musical star called Mimi Crawford, who had become the Dowager Countess of Suffolk. She was beautiful; her late husband, who worked for the Ministry of Supply as a Research Officer, had been awarded a posthumous George Cross for dismantling the most dangerous unexploded bombs. On her visits to King's Mead she was very solicitous of me, a senior prefect. On returning to London she wrote me a charming letter on Savoy paper adorned with a coronet asking me to return her son's confiscated penknife which he had used to carve his way through many desks. I was very impressed by her letter, less so by her son!

There was a great deal of speculation among the boys as to whether these visiting mothers came to see their sons or to meet the good-looking Shilcock, who I don't think was interested in women: he preferred his boys.

Although the Nott family came from a modest background, many other parents were rather grand. Somehow Douglas had established King's Mead as a fashionable school for the sons of the great and the good, especially among the military establishment. Admirals Lord Chatfield and Keyes (the son of the latter was awarded a posthumous Victoria Cross) were often resident as guests – and Lord Trenchard, the founder of the Royal Air Force, sent his sons to King's Mead, too. Admiral Lord Fisher, the famous First Sea Lord who tussled with Churchill, was also a visitor. I include a photograph of an unannounced visit by George V and Queen Mary to the school. The King was recuperating in a home near Eastbourne and his agent at Sandringham suggested that he dropped into this nearby school. It was a shock to the system to have a King and Queen arriving unannounced. The King sniffed the tumblers on the dining table and asked whether the boys drank alcohol! It must have been the servants, Shilcock quickly answered.

Another frequent visitor was a senior lady of the Guinness family. According to Douglas she was never parted from her valuable pearls, which he claimed she wore in bed at night. He generated a competitive spirit among the boys by speculating whether she also wore her pearls in the bath! Another joyful anecdote comes from the train journey from Bideford to Waterloo at the end of term. The train was meant to stop at Basingstoke, which I believe was then the residence of the Colman family of mustard fame. As we entered Basingstoke station, there on the platform was a retinue of servants waiting to meet young Colman, but the train did not oblige: it steamed on through the station without stopping. Much cheering among the boys. It was a happy time.

I met a fellow old boy called Christopher Caroll, a godson of Douglas Shilcock, to learn more about him. His father was a Grenadier and got to know Douglas Shilcock in the trenches at the Battle of Ypres. I don't know anything about Shilcock's parents, but I think they were members of the Church. Both sons became preparatory school headmasters, and there must have been money somewhere as Douglas bought his way into King's Mead in the 1920s and spent large sums on the buildings and facilities thereafter.

Douglas Shilcock wanted to interest his boys in all sorts of experiences outside the school curriculum. He took a group of boys to camp on the last beat on the River Torridge at Rosemoor just below Torrington. Here we explored the river. In those days it was full of freshwater mussels – and it was not too rare to find a freshwater pearl. Douglas had a pearl as his tie pin. Today freshwater mussels have all but disappeared thanks to farm effluent in the rivers. This particular part of the River Torridge was a scene of wonder in Henry Williamson's famous book *Salar the Salmon*. Douglas came down to the river and taught me for the first time to cast a salmon fly. He was also keen to show the boys how poachers tickled salmon, so we spent much time on our stomachs tickling the fish as they rested along the banks of the river.

When the war ended we returned to Seaford. It was my last two years before leaving for public school. I became Head Boy, Captain of Football and Cricket. Never in my life was I again to acquire the power and prestige held by a Head Boy at a preparatory school. Nothing compared with it; there was no debate, no questioning, no democracy: the boys did what they were told, or else. It would have been easier this way with the Admirals and Generals in the Ministry of Defence . . .

I took the Common Entrance exam while my form master Mr Rattray stood over me. Here and there he helped me through the Classics paper. Was it cheating? Possibly. It was a great mistake because I was never academically very bright; and I was put in too high a class when I arrived at my next school. As Captain of Cricket, I was also recommended as a cricket wizard. Alas, again, I never made the team. It was no great loss, as I spent the summer fishing the River Pang.

How do I sum it up? I had a very happy time at King's Mead, at a very difficult time in wartime England. It really set me up for the next seventy-five years. In the holidays, because of evacuation, I had no friends; I was lonely. But at school I made so many friends and ran wild among the woods on the Moreton estate.

Presiding over it all was a rather remarkable headmaster; he must have been good at it to have held the school together for thirty-three years. I get upset when my former colleagues, now mostly passed away, suggest that Douglas was a suppressed homosexual. Maybe, but so what?

One last surprise remains. Out of the blue in 1943 my mother received an invitation to spend Christmas with myself and my sister at the Royal Oak Hotel on Exmoor. My mother was an attractive lady but, as I have said, I am sure Douglas was not interested in women. With her husband away at the war he saw that she was lonely and genuinely wanted to help her during the festivities. It was a simple act of kindness and I see no reason to question his motive. We had a happy uneventful Christmas. So much for Douglas – a good man by any measure.

Chapter Sixteen

Sir David Omand

Civil servant

D avid Omand did not reach the very top of the Civil Service, namely the position of Cabinet Secretary, but he should have done. In the competition for the top post between Andrew Turnbull and himself, Turnbull won out because Tony Blair felt that he had more experience at outmanoeuvring Gordon Brown when he was at the Treasury! While David was Permanent Secretary at the Home Office he contracted cancer and had to step aside. I had recourse to the memoir of Jack Straw, the Home Secretary at the time, and it is clear that David faced several crises which would have tested anyone's health.

When David recovered from cancer he ran the Government Communications Centre (GCHQ) at Cheltenham, possibly the most vital institution defending our national security. He then spent seven years in the Cabinet Office as Permanent Secretary responsible for the coordination and administration of all branches of the Security Services. So he possibly has more knowledge of the administration of security than any other person, politicians and civil servants included. He has written the definitive book, *Securing the State*, about his experiences.

I am a huge admirer of our Civil Service. I spent six years as a Minister and I was supported by three Permanent Secretaries and some six Principal Private Secretaries. On my arrival as Minister of State in the Treasury my Private Secretary, Diana Seaman, told me not to use the telephone on my desk as it was monitored by the Security Services and that her colleague, the Chancellor's Private Secretary, was very self-important and might act as a block in contact with my boss, the Chancellor, Tony Barber. A very inadequate man from MI6 would interview me, but he will be well-meaning, she said! Total loyalty to me, more so than to her department. My Principal Private Secretary in Trade, Stuart Hampson, and his predecessor before him had acted for Hattersley and Shirley Williams just before my arrival after the election, but was utterly loyal to someone holding an entirely different philosophy from his socialist predecessors.

Stuart left the Civil Service prematurely and became a very successful Chairman of the John Lewis Partnership. When I left politics for the City I was often approached by talented civil servants who were so frustrated by government bureaucracy that they wanted to move to the private sector. I warned them against it, as the work of senior civil servants was much more absorbing and varied than anything that they would find there. One who did, Frances Heaton, whom I had known in the Treasury, moved to Lazard, the investment bank, and rose to the top as a director of the Bank of England.

I remember all my Permanent and Private Secretaries in government. I became very dependent on them – and never saw the need to recruit a political adviser. I was the politician; why should I need a political adviser? Today, all Ministers have political advisers who can cause unnecessary tensions in the system. What I needed was an intelligent and loyal adviser to administer and oil the wheels of the Whitehall machine, necessary to get things done in that strange environment.

Having lavished praise on the Civil Service for its independence and integrity, it rather shocked me when three former Cabinet Secretaries, Lords Turnbull, Butler and O'Donnell, launched an attack on critics of the Civil Service by suggesting that MPs who defended the 'Leave' campaign were selling 'snake oil'. One can hardly criticize these gentlemen, freed from the restrictions of the Civil Service Code of Behaviour, for advancing their personal opinion in the House of Lords. But they still occupy positions at the peak of the British establishment, and to those of us who support the vote of the 17.4 million 'Leavers' it seems quite wrong not to back the elected British government in its negotiations with the European Union.

How the Permanent Secretary to the Treasury could ever have endorsed an economic forecast prior to the Referendum that an EU exit would cost households an average of £4,300 a year by 2030 is very hard to see. Since Treasury-led forecasts have been shown to be completely wrong, if not absurd, it is hardly surprising that the Civil Service is accused of bias. The three Cabinet Secretaries – all alumni of the British Treasury in which I served myself – feel a pull of loyalty to a failing institution.

There is an explanation for the failings of the Civil Service in certain circumstances. It cannot handle radicalism; hence its gut opposition to our proposed exit from the EU. The Civil Service is at its best organizing the 'politics of decline', a straightforward management task. Give it a tricky assignment and it retreats into consensus and calls upon inter-departmental committees to come up with solutions. Of course they seldom exist. I don't doubt that the current Civil Service is doing its best to find a diplomatic answer to an apparent impasse with the Commission, but it has this deep fear of change.

I first met David Omand when I arrived in the Ministry of Defence from the Trade Department. He was, I think, No. 2 in my private office. The No. 3, Jonathan Dawson, left the Civil Service and joined Lazard, where he was a very successful director and made a modest fortune. I did not get on very well with the No. 1 in my private office – he understandably found my restlessness very tiresome – so I asked the Permanent Secretary, a rather famous civil servant called Frank Cooper, if he could promote David to No. 1. Frank demurred; he was not senior enough for the post. Promote him then, I said, and it duly happened. I like to think it was the beginning of his ascent to the top of the Civil Service; talent wins out even in that hierarchical environment.

David was my right-hand man and principal supporter in my controversial Defence Review which I discuss in the chapters on Admiral Lewin and Field Marshal Bramall. He was also with me throughout the Falklands campaign, which I found difficult. David is an archetypical civil servant, clever and very practical with it, very patient, quite cautious; he might be accused of being rather uninspiring. In other words, he was the ideal Private Secretary for me because I had none of his qualities, except maybe that I was never dull! Well, they were hard times and he saw me through them.

Of course I discussed the nature of the Civil Service, a very great British institution, with David on several occasions. The famous Fulton Report talked of 'administration' and not of 'management'. The Civil Service was traditionally made up of 'generalists' who had the talent and skill to move from one department to another. The stereotypes of generalists versus specialists, amateurs versus professionals, administrators versus managers, not least gentlemen versus players, had rather dogged the debate ever since Fulton. The quality admired by Ministers in a good civil servant used to be well expressed in a War Office memo: 'Officers should not run, it frightens the horses.' Of course, given the chance, civil servants gather together in inter-departmental committees where nothing gets decided or done. I found it necessary in all departments to persistently enquire what had happened to 'x' and 'y', otherwise they simply disappeared into the system.

The world has changed since Fulton. One of the great weaknesses of the late twentieth century Civil Service was the lack of specialists, such as contract officers, project managers and IT staff, a deficit to which a litany of overspent and failing programmes bear witness. The problem lies in recruiting, because of the very high pay that these skills command in the private sector. I think the Civil Service is rightly suspicious of the idea that the procurement of consultants in these skills is necessarily the answer to the Civil Services' inability to cover the wide range of today's management requirements.

Businessmen do not understand the complexity under which the public sector operates, with hundreds of conflicting voices and complete transparency of everything that happens in government. Since that foolish socialist introduction of the Freedom of Information Act it is impossible to undertake an internal debate on complex issues without it being the subject of malicious probing by journalists and outsiders. It is impossible for a private sector organization and companies to conceive of the intrusiveness under which the Civil Service now operates. It is under intolerable pressure.

Foolish measures by Major and Blair have also damaged the integrity of the Civil Service. And it has got worse under May. Because Major, in particular, found it hard to resist press criticism of parliamentary behaviour, he handed over the policing of elected Parliamentarians to *un*elected senior mandarins, who in their special world share even more prejudices than Prime Ministers – and certainly more than the collective wisdom of cross-party Parliamentarians!

For a hundred years or more, constitutional tradition was clear: only elected politicians should police other politicians. Now we have to suffer endless patronizing pontification from retired mandarins, who are ill-equipped to police elected politicians; nor do they wish to do so.

Rather worse was Blair's decision to put recommendations for the award of honours in the hands of another mandarin committee. It led to criticism in the press suggesting that undue privilege was being granted to Labour Party donors. It used to be called patronage and it is better in the hands of Prime Ministers than unelected civil servants who show no reluctance to award honours to themselves.

These thoughts came to me on 1 January 2018 when I saw that no honour was awarded to the most successful politician of our era, one Nigel Farage. I have never been a supporter or member of UKIP, but I think his exclusion is a disgrace.

This prime ministerial 'cop out' has recently been at its most distasteful and absurd when the Prime Minister Theresa May asked the Civil Service 'ethics' adviser in the Cabinet Office to prepare a report on the alleged misbehaviour of her closest friend and senior politician – Damian Green MP. What on earth has this got to do with the Civil Service? It is not a police force. The Ministerial Code, such as it is, should be policed by a cross-party committee of politicians making recommendations for disciplinary action to the Prime Minister herself.

David being a retiring former civil servant, I wanted to ask him about his early life. So far as I could tell, it had not been published anywhere. He went to Glasgow Academy and then on to Cambridge. He obtained a First in Economics and Statistics at Cambridge in 1969 – ten years after I left Cambridge with a poor Second! Then, having retired, he gained a First in Mathematics and Theoretical Physics in 2008 at the Open University. But the most interesting information that I gleaned from him was his description of the exam that he took as an undergraduate to enter GCHQ at Cheltenham in 1969. I quote from his description:

The GCHQ mind

I was pleased last month to receive a Christmas card from Robert Hannigan, the current Director of GCHQ, containing the fiendish quiz his cryptographers had set. Like everyone else I did not manage to finish all the stages. The puzzle brought back memories of my own recruitment to GCHQ from Cambridge in 1969 when I had to sit their entrance exam in a cold north Cambridge church hall, since formally in those days the existence of GCHQ as an intelligence organization was still secret. It was quite the most difficult exam I had ever experienced. I was interviewed, later discovering it was curiosity on their part as to how someone with a very respectable academic record could have failed to solve all their problems. But they took me on as a young fast streamer nevertheless. And much later when I returned to Cheltenham to be Director I reflected on what we should be looking for in recruiting young graduates today.

Of course a diverse set of skills is needed. Linguists with that extraordinary ability to grasp hard languages. Electronics engineers and today digital natives who have deep understanding of coding and algorithms and the inner workings of the internet. The general qualities needed are, however, part mental and part moral.

For the former, what is so useful is the capacity for sustained thinking, holding a problem in one's mind, examining it from every angle. Helpful here is a good visual memory, even an eidetic memory, of the kind exhibited by the late Hugh Alexander (member of Hut 6 at Bletchley Park); Hugh was Chief Cryptographer at GCHQ in my time and with GCHQ colleagues used to play at lunchtime several chess games simultaneously and blindfolded.

In addition, a strong moral compass is essential for everyone at GCHQ. The officers of all our intelligence agencies have the task of keeping us safe and protecting our national interests. They are equipped with powerful means of achieving that, including in the case of GCHQ the ability to access and search bulk data on the internet for the communications of those who mean us harm, the dictators, terrorists, criminals, hackers, narcotics gangs, proliferators, child abusers, and sadly today people traffickers.

Bitter conflicts such as Bosnia in the 1990s helped to convince Whitehall and Westminster that the Government Communications Centre in

Cheltenham was worth a new investment. As a result, David oversaw the building of the largest secret intelligence headquarters outside the United States. It was the largest new building ever envisaged by a British government and, at the time, the largest construction project in Europe. Everyone was brought together in a new building, holding more than 5,000 personnel, with several hundred miles of fibre optic cabling. Today it is at the leading edge of Britain's struggle against terrorism and organized crime. The root-and-branch reform which David oversaw as the new Director of GCHQ made the whole operation into the most important security operation in the Western world. It is a great achievement.

My own experience of secret intelligence was mainly restricted to Defence Intelligence, although I was a recipient of the so-called Red Book, circulated among a restricted circle of senior ministers on a monthly basis; this was a distillation of intelligence from several quarters and it was prepared by the Joint Intelligence Committee in the Cabinet. David served on the Committee for seven years. I found it inadequate on several counts; the distillation took the sex out of intelligence reports. Churchill, a recipient of this same process, declared that he was not interested in the author's opinion in such a report; he insisted on receiving the raw data. I often found some newspaper reports more intriguing and perceptive than what I was offered by the Whitehall system.

I also discovered that it is very hard for intelligence specialists to curb their enthusiasm for their discoveries. Witness MI6 and Iraq. During my time, at the height of the Cold War, I was frequently approached for a briefing on the latest information provided by satellite SIGINT and wireless intercepts (ELINT). The ability of satellites to follow the smallest activity on the ground was astonishing; we could watch people and vehicles moving around, even through cloud cover. So the specialists were always discovering a new Soviet aircraft carrier being constructed, or movement in a Soviet submarine base. We knew exactly where the Soviets' Command and Control centres were located on the outskirts of Moscow which was the basis for Trident targeting. One of the more distressing elements of this game was to follow Soviet chemical warfare exercises, in which many participants perished. The Soviets knew that we knew what they were up to – and I believe it was an important element in deterrence.

I learned to be very wary of many intelligence briefings which, in retrospect, exaggerated Soviet readiness and the effectiveness of their forces that a decade or two later were in a state of near-collapse. The money to support the Soviet defence programme ran out. Reagan simply outspent the Soviets and bankrupted them. It will happen again to Putin's war machine, which is some eight times underfinanced compared to the Americans. The Russian economy is small, rather smaller than our own, and heavy military expenditure by the Russian state cannot be sustained indefinitely. Unfortunately, the intelligence community is only noticed by governments if it makes startling if somewhat unfounded discoveries. In my case, it was a plea from the intelligence community for us to increase our own defence expenditure to meet the Soviet threat.

David Omand was Security Co-ordinator during the Iraq War, and in his evidence to the Chilcot Committee he said that MI6 intelligence provided by Sir Richard Dearlove to Blair was 'over-promised and under-developed'. Dearlove grew too close to Blair – and Blair became dependent on him.

In *Securing the State* David Omand gives examples of several successes and failures in the use of intelligence. He sums these up by saying, 'The most basic purpose of intelligence is to improve the quality of decision-making by reducing ignorance.'

He mentions, too, the Zimmermann Telegram, which was deciphered by British cryptographers in 1917; the outrage following its publication in the American press contributed to the United States' declaration of war against Germany and its allies. He next gives the example of the Americans in 1941 being in ignorance of the real position of the Japanese aircraft carriers; the United States discounted the possibility of an attack on Pearl Harbor. Being able to control German agents in the UK and read German cipher traffic, the UK was able to mount an effective deception plan that materially reduced the risk of the 1944 Normandy landings. Finally, having secret intelligence on the activity of Al-Qaeda suspects enabled the discovery and disruption in 2006 of a major plot to bring down a number of airliners over the Atlantic.

David Omand and I were personally involved in perhaps one of the most recent failures of intelligence gathering, and it led us to the Falklands War.

In 1982 he and I were in Colorado Springs in the USA for the NATO Nuclear Planning Group. At the height of the Cold War the purchase of the D5 Trident nuclear missile system was uppermost in my mind. It would be fair to say that the initial reports of the Argentinian scrap-metal merchants landing on South Georgia did not get our full attention. In hindsight, it should have done. It was being handled in the Foreign Office.

David gives an account of this in his book:

> I have the enduring memory of working with the Secretary of State in the House of Commons a few days later on his speech to announce the purchase of Trident D5 when specific signals intelligence reports arrived via the Defence Intelligence Staff unambiguously recording that the Argentine military had carried out a beach reconnaissance at landing sites in the Falkland Islands; then the penny did certainly drop, and we raced down the corridors to find Margaret Thatcher in her room to tell her the bad news that having suffered a failure of intelligence assessment, intelligence now indicated an invasion was almost certain, but also that we were initially powerless to stop it.

I don't blame myself for not having enquired more vigorously into the consequences of the peaceful Argentinian landing on South Georgia; I was personally transfixed with getting our controversial proposals for Trident D5 through the House of Commons the week after our meetings in Colorado Springs. I did telephone from America during the meeting, but was told that the Argentinian scrap merchants had taken down the flag and were departing! Oh well. Such is life!

I must conclude this chapter by describing how David Omand helped to devise the 'Contest' strategy for counter-terrorism when he was in the Cabinet Office Whatever criticism can be levelled at the tribal nature of our armed forces, at one thing they are superb. David as my Private Secretary, and later as the Senior Deputy Under-Secretary for Policy, must have absorbed over several years the passion for risk planning in that organization. As Erwin Rommel famously said, 'Before the battle is fought, it is decided by the quartermaster.' Indeed, the planning by

Admiral Fieldhouse in his bunker in north London to organize the logistics for the Falklands campaign was superb. And as Frank Cooper, the former Permanent Secretary at the Ministry of Defence, once said to me when I expressed scepticism about how we could overcome the logistic problem of the Falklands, 'You must understand, John, that the one thing that the military are really good at is getting equipment and people from A to B.'

So David, after the trauma of 9/11 and the bombing on the London Underground on 7/2, set out in the Cabinet Office to devise what became known as the four Ps on counter-terrorism: Pursue, Prevent, Protect, Prepare. At that time, too, the British government, under Blair, doubled its expenditure on the Security Services.

We must be very wary of any attempt to prevent the Security Services from carrying out the limited intrusion into our civil liberties that is essential for them to gather intelligence, primarily through GCHQ in Cheltenham. I remember well the astounding skill used by intelligence services in Northern Ireland to infiltrate the IRA, using every kind of human signal and electronic intelligence to undermine its confidence and morale. Some of the methods used might have been provocative to liberal opinion, but it led to the collapse of terrorism and the end of killing in that province.

So the task of risk planning is to create a state of confidence on the part of the public that the major risks, be they malign threats or natural hazards, are being satisfactorily managed so that people can get on with making the most of their lives in confidence. We owe it to the Civil Service planners, and in particular to David Omand, that life still continues, more or less freely, in spite of a major threat to our existence.

Chapter Seventeen

Sir Ian Fraser

Soldier, journalist, banker

W hy is it that, when you read about successful people in books, the most interesting time is their early years? This particularly applies to politicians who may even have risen to be Premier, Foreign Secretary or Chancellor. It is not that history in the making as influenced by successful politicians is dull – far from it – but the lives of distinguished persons before they become prominent has a special fascination. This is the case with Ian Fraser.

Ian was born in 1923 and brought up in the 600-year-old Moniack Castle on the River Beauly, on the outskirts of Inverness. A scion of the Lovat Fraser clan, his upbringing as a member of a rather poor aristocratic family was dominated by history and its connections with other Scottish clans. His father, the fifth son of the 14th Lord Lovat, was wounded at Gallipoli. His cousin 'Shimi' Lovat was a renowned commando in the Second World War; David Stirling, the founder of the SAS, was another cousin; and Veronica Fraser married Fitzroy Maclean, yet another hero. The Frasers are a warrior race.

Inevitably, as a young man he joined the Scots Guards in the middle of the war, only to find himself at Salerno, from where he escaped but was then caught up in horrid conditions in the Apennines in northern Italy, where he won a Military Cross in the last few months of the Second World War.

In his memoir Ian describes the appalling life in his unit's slit trenches from October to the end of February 1945: 'The cold, the wet, the endless nagging fear of death or mutilation are memories that will never leave any of us who went through that dreadful winter in the Apennines.' Initially, his platoon was under constant attack and bombarded by the German artillery:

> Our searchlights lit up two miles to the north of us. In this way
> the coal-scuttle helmets of the Germans coming over the brow

towards us were well illuminated. Several of the men blazed away, Stewart, Morrison, Sangster and Charlie Wright. After a couple of hours, the Germans withdrew leaving four or five men dead in front of us. I shot two distant Germans with my rifle which I handled as if I was stalking in the Highlands.

I must mention here Ian's astonishing memory for people. He wrote an outstanding autobiography, *The High Road to England*. Throughout this fascinating story he seems to have remembered the names of every one of his contemporaries right through his life, and particularly the names of the individual Guardsmen who served in his platoon. 'I loved them', he says. At the age of ten he had been sent away to Ampleforth and then on to Magdalen College, Oxford. At school, he wrote, 'I met the future Cardinal Basil Hume. The school numbered a marquis, and an ambassador among my contemporaries as well as one who went to prison, one who died of drugs and one eaten by savages.' But his law studies at Oxford were interrupted by the war, although his tutor, A. J. P. Taylor, said that he would have gained a First. This does not surprise me, for in the ten or more years that I worked with him in the City he struck me as having an outstanding brain.

On leaving the Army in 1945, Ian joined Reuters and went on to become their chief correspondent in Bonn, the capital of the brand new Federal Republic of Germany. A new nation was being born, and Ian read A. J. P. Taylor's famous books about Germany: 'Nationalism had arrived late in Germany,' wrote Taylor, 'and when it came at the turn of the 18th century, it focussed more on the unification of Germany, the land of poets and thinkers than on the re-constitution of the Holy Roman Empire, as represented by Bismarck and Prussia.' As a young journalist Ian was deeply involved in, and an admirer of, the new Germany. A recent platoon commander of thirty men, he met several of Hitler's generals, Manstein, Manteuffel, and in particular Kesselring, who had commanded the German army in Italy. It is hardly surprising that journalism holds a special place in the ambitions of intelligent young men.

Among his many experiences in Germany was his encounter with Robert Maxwell, in a pink Chrysler, smuggling contraband across the border from East to West using a false press pass from the *Jewish Chronicle*.

He could not publish this story for fear of libel, but he was to encounter Maxwell again in later years.

After ten years with Reuters, having served in Paris, Berlin and Bonn, he was introduced to Siegmund Warburg (see Chapter Two). Still in his thirties, he joined Warburgs as a young trainee. He spoke and wrote fluent German, as well as French and Italian, but he became restless about the diminishing powers of the founders of the firm, only to be recruited by the Prime Minister and Governor of the Bank of England to establish better control of the City's behaviour, especially in the field of takeovers.

The body concerned was known as the City Panel on Takeovers & Mergers, and Ian turned it into a major force in controlling the piratical practices of the City's merchant banks seeking to win contests on behalf of their industrial clients. 'The takeover business,' he said, 'had become an area of complete lawlessness inhabited by cowboys.'

The Panel, which controlled, by voluntary agreement, disputes between contestants, came across a bid by an American company called Leasco for Robert Maxwell's Pergamon Press. When Leasco examined Pergamon Press they discovered several accounting irregularities and sought to withdraw their offer. Fraser ruled that Leasco could do this, which prompted furious threats by Maxwell to sue him. It went to an appeal, chaired by Sir Hartley Shawcross, at which Maxwell indulged in all sorts of histrionics, including sobbing into a large handkerchief. The huge publicity surrounding this affair firmly established the Panel's authority for the first time.

Here I have to tell of my own experience with Robert Maxwell many years later. I was de facto Chairman of a new newspaper called the *Sunday Correspondent*. It was failing. I needed to arrange fresh capital to keep it alive, and I offered the printing contract to Maxwell's company in return for an investment in the newspaper. I visited Maxwell in his suite at the top of the *Daily Mirror* building. As a fellow ex-Parliamentarian Maxwell greeted me effusively, although I hardly knew him.

'How much do you want?' asked Maxwell.

'Five million pounds,' I replied.

'That should not be a problem,' said Maxwell, at which point a butler appeared and said, 'Excuse me, Mr Maxwell, Mr Gorbachev is on the telephone and wants to speak to you.'

'Excuse me,' said Maxwell, 'the First Secretary is always seeking my advice.'

Of course it was invented theatre. I am sure that Gorbachev did not call Maxwell. No doubt he thought that it would impress his visitor. The practices of intense flattery, name-dropping and a pretence of good connections seem to be a speciality of Jewish businessmen. They do not impress Englishmen, but I experienced them, particularly in Warburgs, and on several visits to the Jewish business community in New York.

When Ian left the City Panel he did not return to Warburgs but was recruited by Lord Poole, the former Chairman of the Conservative Party and Chief Executive of Pearsons, to liven up the bank of Lazard, a competitor of Warburgs; the two rather despised each other. The Governor of the Bank of England, Robin Leigh-Pemberton, tried to recruit him to lead the City as a major regulator and plied him with a knighthood, even suggesting that a peerage might be organized if he took the job.

'I mumbled something about there being already too many peers in the Fraser clan for this to have any magnetic attraction for me – and the conversation ended there,' said Ian.

He was not a snob but was intensely proud of his Scottish heritage; he felt painfully the tragic collapse of the Lovat dynasty, forced to sell everything in the Highlands because of a series of deaths and mismanagement.

So he came to Lazard, which undoubtedly had the best connections and the longest list of major industrial clients in the City. But it was asleep. Lazard represented the 'old' City, the traditional English way of doing things, before Warburgs successfully challenged this in the 1960s. Ian Fraser and I had both been educated by Siegmund Warburg, who despised Lord Kindersley of Lazard, the Chairman of Hambros and the Chairman of Morgan Grenfell, Lord Bicester, of whom it was said in his eightieth year, 'Rufie is not very bright but we all like doing business with him.'

This questioning of English ways was fortified in Ian Fraser by his experience as a journalist in France and Germany, where he absorbed the continental way of looking at England – and it was not complimentary. England was going downhill fast in the days of 'managed decline' so well represented by that paternalistic actor Harold Macmillan. Ian Fraser wrote in his memoir:

> [Macmillan's view of a declining country] caused much distress at home. My beloved Mama brought up in the traditions of High Anglican Toryism, thought or rather knew that British was best . . . I however knew, with the exuberance of youth and my new self-confidence, that I ridiculed many of these established views of England . . . The Germans and the French thought our country was the dirtiest, our slums the nastiest and our industry the most inefficient in Europe, furthermore our food was disgusting and our national diet of potato chips and Mars bars meant that we have the worst teeth in the Western world. But what really riled the womenfolk at home was when I held forth on the growing insignificance of England in the eyes of the Americans, the French, and Germans.

I shared this view of my country in the 1960s and it determined the views of the early Thatcher generation.

To wake up Lazard was no small task, and I only talk about it because the modern generation has no idea how bad things were in the City in Macmillan's England – not so long before the Thatcher revolution. Ian recruited another former colleague from Warburgs called Bernard Kelly, and these two made themselves unpopular. The directors of Lazard, whose board had consisted of four peers under the chairmanship of Lord Hamden, were unprepared to change their ways and seek out new business. Three of the largest UK companies were clients – BP, Unilever and BAT – and Daniel Meinertzhagen, who preceded Ian Fraser as Chairman, had said of possible new clients, 'They know where we are and if they want our services they will come to our door.' Ian took on the men he described as the 'Four Colonels', who had the chairmanship of several leading companies. He says that they were seldom in the office and when they arrived, 'They seemed to spend their time dictating letters to their Lazard secretaries about their outside companies or the management of their country estates.' The Four Colonels, all of whom had fine wartime records, eventually retired and Ian succeeded Meinertzhagen as Chairman. By the time I arrived, having been hunted down from politics by Bernard Kelly and Ian Fraser, Lazard had recruited a team of younger, intelligent men and it was thriving. When Ian retired in poor health, I took over the chairmanship from him. I gave a description of the differences between Warburgs and Lazard in my memoir, *Here Today, Gone Tomorrow*.

I do not think that Ian Fraser's retirement went very happily. His beloved wife, Ann, dropped dead of a heart attack at the age of forty; she was a compulsive smoker. He retired to a farm in Somerset and spent his time fighting the Lloyds establishment that had bankrupted many landowners. He married again, Fiona Douglas-Home, a niece of Sir Alec, the former Conservative Prime Minister. I visited him in Somerset; he was not in a good way. It is so sad that a remarkable man, with a brilliant brain, somewhat austere but often great fun and charming, should have suffered a rather lonely old age. I owe a great deal to Ian and Bernard Kelly who persuaded me to leave politics at exactly the right time. And while I am not sure the City was always the right place for me, it has provided me with a comfortable old age.

Chapter Eighteen

Lord Hurd

Politician

I was beastly to Douglas when he was Foreign Secretary. I regret it. I had already left politics, and I found myself in passionate opposition to the government's handling of the Bosnian War and the Maastricht Treaty.

My wife was deeply committed to the Bosnian Muslims, who were being murdered by Serb irregulars attached to the Yugoslav army; this led remorselessly to the massacre at Srebrenica. I thought that the Major government and the Foreign Office should have taken a firmer line against Milošević, but appeasement was the chosen policy of the diplomatic community.

I wrote several articles in the press, levying criticism at the Foreign Office on both these issues. It was disloyal, if you like, to my Party and my former colleagues; although, having left politics, I felt no loyalty to the Major government

When Douglas Hurd wrote his memoirs, it was natural that the *Guardian* should have asked me, a critic of Douglas, to review his book.

Although we were very different politicians, holding quite opposing views on many issues, I tried to be fair to him in my review. Douglas was always a moderate seeking out 'the centre ground'. I was always a radical, against consensus politics. These two extracts of what we wrote about each other are quite interesting in showing up the central philosophical division in the Conservative Party – an example of the broad church in which we operated. Mine first:

Jeeves at the FO

Douglas Hurd was always measured, detached, a safe pair of hands, writes John Nott. In short, the perfect butler – as his Memoirs *attest.*

Memoirs
by Douglas Hurd
544pp, Little, Brown, £20

It is a matter of regret to me that I was never a close colleague of
Douglas Hurd. Although he is two years older than I am, he entered
parliament rather late at the age of 43, after a distinguished career as a
junior diplomat and as Ted Heath's political secretary. I was gone before
he reached the cabinet. My regret at never having known him well is all
the greater for having read this admirable memoir.

Much of Hurd's life seems to have been devoted to winning prizes;
he was a king's scholar at Eton, captain of the school, a scholar at Trinity,
Cambridge, where he went on to get first-class honours in History.
Eventually he obtained the greatest prize of all, at least for him – the
foreign secretaryship. I suspect that, although he reached his goal with
pride and satisfaction, it somehow never quite lived up to his – or is it
our? – expectations. Maybe this was no fault of his. 'Events, dear boy,
events' crowded in on him: the quarrels over the Maastricht treaty, the
first Gulf war, the departure from Hong Kong and, worst of all, the
ghastly Bosnian dilemma – surely one of the most shaming episodes in
recent British history.

But it was a triumph in this strange country of ours to surmount his
boyhood brilliance to become the very model of an elder statesman; to be
the head boy, the school swot who refused to disappear into anonymity in
later life; a highly unusual if not unique achievement.

If his memoir has avoided most of the pitfalls of political autobiography, it is because it is more of a personal journey than a list of
political achievements. We have to wade through an awful lot of summits,
handshakes, group photographs, dinners and anecdotes of great men
met and analysed, but the catalogue is rescued by the reflections of a
civilised man.

I never understand why most of us enjoy reading about the great
events of history, and are prepared to follow patiently the political
shenanigans that go on day by day, but find it hard to enjoy the intermediate
form of history represented by the political memoir. Perhaps it is because
the politicians find their time in government so totally absorbing that

they are desperate to transmit their experience to others. They normally fail to do so. Politicians don't read each others' memoirs; they simply consult the index to see what the author says about them.

The best part of these memoirs – indeed all political memoirs – is the early life. Hurd writes about his upbringing on a farm in Wiltshire with great warmth. He gives very moving descriptions of the death of his beloved brother, and the sickness and recovery of his wife Judy; his analysis of the character and achievements of Margaret Thatcher is brilliant, as is his description of life as a young diplomat in Beijing, New York, Rome and London (intense activity, occasional excitement and prolonged periods of boredom, just like being in the army).

Reading about his time as a diplomat, I wondered whether he took the wrong fork in the road when he left the Foreign Service to become a politician. Hurd would have been an outstanding permanent under-secretary, but he will not go down as a great foreign secretary.

His popular image is that of a rather cold, aloof patrician. It is unfair, but it persists. I think it was a sergeant-major in the army who chastised him for holding himself like a butler on parade – he was right. There is something of the good butler about Douglas Hurd – measured, detached, correct, always a safe pair of hands. Butlers must never be inspired, emotional, passionate. One wants occasionally to find Hurd smashing china, tipping soup down a dowager's cleavage, but it never happens.

The 15th Earl of Derby became foreign secretary in 1866. The son of a conservative, he was a liberal in everything he did. He compared his conduct in that great post 'to that of a man floating down a river and fending off from his vessel, as well as he could, the various obstacles he encountered'. It is a good description of how the British Foreign Office sees its function, and a junior diplomat who becomes foreign secretary is unlikely to break the mould. I believe that every foreign secretary needs a strong prime minister. It is dangerous to leave the Foreign Office to its own devices – to pursue its sole purpose in life, diplomacy, the building of a consensus with people like Slobodan Milošević who do not understand the word. It leads, always, to appeasement.

Thatcher and Blair brought clout to the Foreign Office. Major certainly did not. The Major government was dominated not by a strong prime minister, but by a triumvirate of obstinate, intellectually arrogant and determined men – Hurd, Clarke and Heseltine. I am sure that Major, whose political instincts were often quite sound, constantly deferred to the intellect of Hurd and Clarke, and sometimes to a cavalry man called Heseltine. All three must take their share of responsibility for the Tory catastrophe of 1997.

Hurd introduces his memoirs by emphasising that he is not a 'hater'. I am sure that it's true of individuals. He is courteous and generous by nature. But he seems to hate what he calls the 'sour right'. I don't think that he regards Thatcher, Tebbit and Lawson as members of that club, but in the penultimate paragraph of the book he says 'the grip of the sour right of the Tory party since 1997 and more especially of the Conservative press has, I believe, prevented the natural turn of the wheel in our favour'. I expect that readers of the Guardian will agree with him. I do not. I think the problem lies with Hurd and his liberal, Eurocentric friends. Hurd is a Whig, not a Tory. But none of this detracts from my admiration for an excellent and very personal account of what 100 years from now, will appear a fascinating period of our history.

John Nott was Secretary of State for Defence 1981–83
Guardian, 11 October 2003

Now for Douglas on me:

Nott's landing
Douglas Hurd on the memoirs of a sharp MP: Here Today, Gone Tomorrow *by John Nott*

Here Today, Gone Tomorrow
by John Nott
350pp, Politico's £20

John Nott's memoirs catch fire during two episodes of his early life. After National Service he served with the Gurkhas in Malaya during the communist emergency. He describes vividly the hazards of a jungle patrol, and does not omit the bars and brothels of Singapore.

Not surprisingly, after the army he found Cambridge boring – until he met his wife, Miloska, whose importance in his life breathes through the whole book. His next adventure, shrewdly described, was with the upcoming merchant bank, Warburgs. Equipped with these varied experiences, he became Member of Parliament for St Ives in 1966.

We tend to fall into a fashionable memory of political events, which begins with press cuttings and is then tossed lazily from one book to another. Nott brings his awkwardly sharp mind to bear on several of these accepted ideas and forces us to rethink. He does not follow the usual alignments. For example, he believes that Ted Heath was justified in sacking Enoch Powell for his immigration speech in 1968; but he hails Powell as the essential author of the free-market doctrine elaborated through the Economic Dining Club of Tory MPs. Nott, disillusioned by his experiences as a Treasury minister under Ted Heath, was a fervent radical in economic matters, but he dismayed Margaret Thatcher by failing to support the proposed Treasury cuts in the Cabinet crisis of July 1981. After that, he found that the Number 10 press machine often briefed against him. He roundly criticises this practice under Thatcher and Blair, but acknowledges that it was inconceivable under prime ministers of whom in general he disapproves, namely Heath and Major.

Nott is scathing about the 'wets' in early Thatcher days and misunderstands why they worried about the course which the party was taking. It is true that most of them were not experts in economic policy, but they were right to be concerned about the reputation for uncaring harshness that Thatcher allowed to build around her government. Major managed to modify this impression sufficiently to grab an unexpected victory in 1992, but it helped to overwhelm the Tories in 1997 and again in 2001. The wheel turns; the present Conservative leadership, against expectations, is again groping towards a new definition of the middle ground.

Nott describes at length his differences with the Royal Navy once he became defence secretary, but then stresses the crucial influence that Sir Henry Leach's self-confidence about the navy had on Thatcher's determination to retake the Falklands, sweeping aside Nott's initial hesitations. Again he corrects a fashionable view, arguing that the French were more effective allies than the Americans at the crucial points of the conflict.

Nott writes attractively throughout. During these political passages and his later analysis of the City, his judgement is authoritative. So it is all the more startling that on the institutions that enrage him, the quality of thought drops down to the level of a tabloid columnist on an off day. Matters that inflame and therefore weaken his judgement include the Germans, the BBC, supermarkets, any talk of coalition, the European Union and above all the Foreign Office. Nott's quick, authoritative temperament is by nature averse to diplomacy. Patience and politeness are indeed only secondary virtues, but perhaps more useful than he acknowledges.

Nott is well aware of his own shortcomings, though they do not seem to depress him. He was not an easy colleague, and made speeches way outside party policy, to the embarrassment of colleagues who actually had the responsibility. He possessed the charm to give the wounded colleague a drink and make amends – though one knew there would be a next time. He is straight, very intelligent and on occasions, when casting off his general air of boredom and detachment, he shows flashes of charm. However, like most people, I have suffered from his boorish behaviour. Nott's description of Ted Heath is not a bad fit for himself. A government needs one or two John Notts – but not too many if it wants to continue in one piece.

Lord Hurd is a former Conservative Foreign Secretary.
Guardian, 30 March 2002

I should conclude by saying that Douglas's criticism of my character is well judged!

I wondered as I concluded this chapter on Douglas Hurd whether, as a 'lapsed tabloid journalist', I could set out my views here about the House of Lords, of which Douglas was an ideal member. More so, he was made Chairman of the Committee which vetted applicants for that once distinguished institution and he served on the Royal Commission for Reform in 1997. Unfortunately, I have not been able to debate this subject with him. So, without any of the inhibitions of a tabloid journalist

I thought that I would set out my view here. Somehow it fits in a chapter about Douglas.

It is clear – and agreed by most peers themselves – that the House of Lords has become an overpopulated absurdity. How can it be sensible for a second chamber to contain approaching as many delegates as the Congress of the People's Republic of China?

There are arguments for a second chamber in the United Kingdom to examine and scrutinize proposals for legislation that comes to it from the elected House of Commons. But it would be possible for this function to be undertaken by a core of, say, 100 elected peers whose role would be to keep the machinery of government running smoothly.

So far as the 800 appointed peers are concerned, the problem always arises as to how it is possible to get agreement to a reform which affects their interests and personal comfort. 'Turkeys do not vote for Christmas.' The current payment for attendance should be abolished. Membership would decline by 50 per cent overnight! The House of Lords has become an 'old people's home' with benefits. Instead, membership of the Lords, numbering, say, 300 peers, should be organized on a five-year circulating basis from distinguished local councillors, senior members of professional bodies, and judges, not unlike today's arrangement for the bishops. These peers would draw no cash for attendance as it would be financed by councils and professional bodies, possibly allowing for travelling expenses, but no more.

I wonder what Douglas would have thought about this outrageous proposal of removing the £300 a day 'benefit' from today's peers. I think he might have agreed with me.

Chapter Nineteen

Lord Bramall

Field Marshal

Dwin Bramall is a man of remarkable physical and especially moral courage. What the police put him through would have destroyed most men, but he is still full of energy and mentally alert at ninety-five.

For me it is his genius for getting along with people, handling people, the manner in which he approaches them and engages them that marks him out. I have met several retired officers who still talk about a booklet that he wrote in Malaya in 1966 when he was commanding the 2nd Battalion of the Royal Green Jackets; it was a lecture on leadership 'the Green Jacket Way', telling the young officer, straight out of Sandhurst, how he should adapt his approach to the new military environment in which he found himself, how he should get along with his soldiers and his fellow officers.

He has published lectures on 'Generals and Generalship', on Field Marshals Haig and Montgomery, but it is his approach to young officers and simple soldiers that should be a lesson to anyone in the military or private industry – to anyone who seeks to influence, persuade and cajole others to his views and patterns of behaviour.

I got to know Dwin well when he was Chief of the General Staff, Head of the Army, during my time 'as his boss', as he describes it. At that time he was to some extent overshadowed by Admiral Lewin, who preceded him as Chief of the Defence Staff. Lewin was a different character, quieter and more reserved. But Dwin, while modest in a way, was not averse to patronizing politicians who did not accept his way of looking at things. He was personally hurt when my successor, Michael Heseltine, concealed from him proposals for reorganizing the top ranks of the military. I think Heseltine's changes were mistaken, but he was correct in hiding his ideas from the Chief of the Defence Staff until they were nearly ready for publication. Anyone who has tried to influence the Chiefs of Staff would know that it was, and maybe still is, an institution plagued by internal differences. Dwin's own book, *The Chiefs* (1992), relates the long history of dispute between the Chiefs of Staff and their political masters. It is an important publication.

I do not want this chapter to be a panegyric, and Dwin would not expect it to be. I differ from him profoundly on his rejection of the nuclear deterrent, and I have never quite understood how such an intelligent man can divorce himself from the necessary requirements of strong defence, with the money to pay for it. Perhaps it is not the task of a general to concern himself with the funding of defence; maybe he should just set out what defence requires – or his personal view of what defence requires – and then leave it to government to work out how to meet it. But I still find it odd.

Among the most pleasant memories of my time in the Ministry of Defence are the several times I spoke at length to the Joint Services Staff College at Shrivenham. It was enormously satisfying to debate defence policy with middle-ranking officers – colonels, commanders, group captains and above – of all three services; the audience always displayed a flexibility and understanding of the dilemmas in defence policy that was absent in the politicking of the Chiefs of Staff.

Where I first understood Dwin was not in the Ministry of Defence at all, but when I saw him operating with soldiers; the trouble that he took to know their names, their family connections, their interests. It all required a lot of homework and a good memory for faces – he worked at all his relationships from the sovereign down. I think it was his special talent for relationships that got him to the top of his profession, added to his understanding and promotion of the Army's tribal instincts.

He was always considerate, charming and helpful to me, but he found it difficult to accept that, although I started life as a regular soldier, somehow his political boss did not look the part! Several times he expressed his surprise that I did not possess appropriate features for a Defence Secretary. In Michael Tillotson's biography of Dwin I am described as follows: 'Skinny, bald and with large black spectacles, he looked what he was – a merchant banker'. Actually, most merchant bankers were much better looking than me – many almost soldier-like in appearance. In *The Chiefs* Dwin himself describes me as 'the gaunt, ascetic figure who replaced Francis Pym when the incompatibility of [Thatcher's] defence and monetary policies was beginning to show'. I was, further:

> The politically ambitious merchant banker who had once served with the Gurkhas, and was Secretary of Trade. He was tasked to take a tougher line than Pym and to clean up what was seen in Whitehall as a financial Augean Stable within the Ministry of Defence. Moreover he was a man in a political and intellectual hurry. Like Sandys he set off on whirlwind tours of military establishments seeking panaceas. Like Healey he called for innumerable studies in a twelve-week breakneck exercise to clear his mind on the issues at stake.

'Seeking panaceas?'

All of this is rather inaccurate. I was never especially politically ambitious, unlike Heseltine, my successor. I was never tasked by the Prime Minister to take a tougher line than Pym. She never mentioned it. When I arrived, a moratorium on all defence expenditure was in place, causing dismay in the Ministry of Defence and great problems with British industry. The Chiefs of Staff, not Pym, created this problem by competing with one another to enhance their own equipment programmes way beyond the capacity of the country to pay for them. The Royal Navy's was the most overextended programme of the three services, and whoever had been in my place would have needed to cut it back. In fact, we increased the Navy programme, without nuclear weapons, by half a billion pounds during my time; it was the forward order programme that needed trimming.

Although this is somewhat out of context, I asked Dwin how he had allowed today's new carrier programme to go forward when he chaired the Chiefs of Staff Committee.

'It is a disaster,' he said.

'Why couldn't you and your colleagues have argued against it?' I asked.

'It was the fault of Prime Minister Gordon Brown, who wanted the carriers to be built in his parliamentary constituency,' he replied.

It was always the politicians' responsibility, not the Chiefs'. Now they complain that the Ministry of Defence has run out of money again. It never occurs to the Chiefs that they hold responsibility for the financial problems.

Some retired naval officers find it hard to be polite to me. I cut back the frigate force to fifty; due to expenditure on the two big carriers it is now down to nineteen, and completely inadequate. We have no frigate force of any consequence. The former Chief of Defence Staff, a later successor to Dwin, Air Chief Marshal Jock Stirrup, a fast-jet fighter pilot in his youth, advised David Cameron on the F35 joint strike fighter programme – each aircraft costing over $100 million. The Norwegians estimate its full life cost at $800 million per aircraft! We cannot afford a full contingent for the two carriers, let alone fully equip the RAF. Now it seems we cannot afford the Army. There is this disconnect among senior officers between their desired equipment and its cost.

Unpublished at the time, there was an internal debate within the Royal Navy as to whether the new carrier programme would undermine the Navy because of its concentration on two hugely expensive carriers with all the necessary supporting air defence, submarine and escorting frigates; would it perhaps have been better to concentrate on a more broadly based Navy with multi-purpose frigates, helicopter carriers and assault ships? To be fair, no one foresaw that the F35 joint strike fighters would cost around $100 million apiece.

At the heart of planning lies the deeply embedded prejudice in the Navy against relying on the RAF to protect carriers at sea, although with today's reach of land-based aircraft this would be no problem. The Navy's experience in the Second World War tells them that they can only rely on their own Fleet Air Arm to defend ships at sea, although now Royal Navy and RAF pilots train together. It is not for me to contest this claim, because I understand it.

At the time of writing, only fourteen aircraft have been delivered and all are currently based in the United States. The cost is crippling and the carriers can hardly ever have a full complement of this aircraft.

Unfortunately, the Royal Navy took the wrong turning, urged on by the voluble Admiral West and successive First Sea Lords, who felt that the Navy's prestige was committed to the carrier programme. The cost has proved a disastrous decision for the Defence programmes generally.

Responsibility also lies with Air Chief Marshal Jock Stirrup, who killed the Harrier in favour of the joint strike fighter. It is undoubtedly an exciting aircraft; in exercises in the United States it has had a kill ratio against the F16 of fifteen to one.

Would it not have been better to continue with the smaller carriers and attempt an upgrade of the Harrier? This was opposed by Jock Stirrup, and the Harriers were scrapped, or sold off to the US Marine Corps. Naval ambition sabotaged any cheaper option, and the three other Chiefs of Staff were not able to stand up against the Navy. So it goes on. I would never have agreed to the big carrier programme. But now that we have them, I wish them and the Royal Navy and all those who serve in them every success in their deployment.

Today's problems are not, of course, Dwin's responsibility, but as a historian I wish that he would recognize how we get ourselves repeatedly into such a mess. Speeches in the House of Lords about the deficiencies of our defences do not solve the problem. It is a cultural gap, actually; an understanding that money counts between the military and their political masters.

What will Dwin be remembered for? So universal are the plaudits in the Army for this rather special General that it would be invidious of me to comment on his distinguished military career, spanning forty years in many important positions: Staff Colonel to Mountbatten when he was seeking the reorganization of Defence as Chairman of the Chiefs of Staff; Commander of 1st British Corps in post-war Germany; Battalion Commander of the Green Jackets in Borneo and in other key appointments. From his youth he was destined for the top.

I talked to him about his experience as a young officer following the landings in Normandy, where he was the only survivor of a German shell which killed all four of his colleagues as they sheltered under an armoured personnel carrier. He went on to win a Military Cross in a later battle on the Belgian/German border. He was a brave soldier and he saw it all in battle. I often wonder how Dwin's generation can have survived the horrors of the war, including what he saw in the devastation of Hiroshima, and still have made a happy peacetime life, in Dwin's case with a particularly lovely wife, Avril.

I have to get one personal comment out of the way and, of course, it will be disputed. I saw him as a fighting soldier, but never as a 'fighting' general. I am not sure that he had the dash, ruthlessness and imagination of a Montgomery, Patten or Allenby. He is more of an Alexander or a Wavell, and I think he might even have made a good successor to Wavell as Viceroy of India; he would certainly have done the job more sensitively than his former boss, Mountbatten. I encountered many generals in my time – some when I was a young ADC to generals in the Army during the Malayan Emergency. My choice for a fighting general during my time in the MoD would have been Bagnall or Chapple.

If I take Field Marshal Wavell as an example, he will be remembered for his books and his writing. I do not remember Wavell as Commander-in-Chief in the Middle East, or even as Viceroy of India, but he will never be forgotten for his anthology of poems, *Other Men's Flowers*, and for his book, *Allenby: A Study of Greatness*. These will be on people's shelves long after his military career is forgotten. Similarly, Dwin's book, *The Chiefs*, and his many speeches in the House of Lords, published in 2017 as *The Bramall Papers: Reflections in War and Peace*, will be a point of reference for historians who want to research the issues that concerned us in the decades after the Second World War and then later in the Cold War. Dwin saw the one as a young brave officer and the other as a general cast into the politics of the day.

So let me examine the politics of the day.

I have tried to follow Dwin's conversion from support to opposition to nuclear deterrence, with Trident. It is an odd conversion for someone who once commanded 1st British Corp in Germany facing up to the overwhelming conventional forces of the Soviet Union. He says circumstances have changed, but we are on a forty-year timescale here. Won't they change again? In his published paper as an emerging student of the Imperial Defence College, and in a speech at All Souls, Oxford, organized by the great Professor Sir Michael Howard, it is hard to detect at that time any clear opposition to the nuclear deterrent. If anything, his views were obscure.

His changed view was very well explained in his valedictory address to the House of Lords in January 2013. 'Now', he said, 'after deep thought' he could not see the 'usefulness' of Trident. I agree that it is certainly not, and never has been, a war-fighting weapon. With him, I agree it is hard to see how the deterrent can ever be 'used', but that is not its purpose. It can only be understood by its impact on the psychology of those who seek to do us terminal harm – maybe in forty years' time. Trident is always there, hidden undiscovered somewhere in the oceans of the world, a warning to nuclear states like Russia, North Korea, Pakistan or Israel that we have the means to retaliate, although, God help us, it is not our policy ever to do so. I can have no confidence that one day we will not be facing again the same threat which we faced from the Soviet Union in the Cold War.

The scepticism of the Army, going back to the foolish opposition of General Carver, is misplaced. I have always harboured the suspicion that the Generals imagine that abolition of Trident would release more money for their tanks, guns and soldiers. That is not the way of Whitehall; the money saved would be grabbed by the Treasury, and we would all be immeasurably weaker for it. If we forfeited the replacement of Trident now, we could never bring it back – and I do not know what the world will look like over the next forty years.

I have several anecdotes about my experience with Dwin, but only one of them is worth recording. It was in my memoir. It arose early in the Falklands campaign, which the Navy were determined to make their show. I asked Admiral Lewin why we didn't send another brigade to add to the trained Commando brigade already embarked and travelling in their landing craft.

'We will see how it develops,' said Lewin. 'I will talk to Admiral Leach.'

Subsequently, the decision was taken by the Chiefs to send 5 Brigade from the Army. Bramall came to see me. The following conversation took place:

NOTT: Who are you intending to send, Dwin?

BRAMALL: We will send the 5th Brigade at Aldershot, but as it has lost two parachute battalions which are already party of the Commando Brigade's landing force, I will supplement it by two Guards battalions.

NOTT: Where are the Guards battalions now?

BRAMALL: I am taking the Scots Guards and the Welsh Guards off ceremonial duties in London.

NOTT: But how can you do that? They will be hopelessly unfit. Haven't you got other infantry battalions available which are already fit and well trained?

BRAMALL: I am sending them this weekend to the Welsh mountains for a period of concentrated battlefield training – they will be fine at the end of it.

NOTT: Oh! Which is the third battalion making up the Brigade strength?

BRAMALL: The 7th Gurkhas who are already part of the 5th Brigade.

NOTT: Dwin, you can't send the Gurkhas. We are having frightful trouble holding things together in the United Nations and it is more than likely that the Indians will kick up a frightful fuss. It is just too risky politically to send the Gurkhas in my view.

BRAMALL: The 7th Gurkhas are part of the 5th Brigade, the designated strategic reserve, and if we recoil from sending them now there will always be some reason for not sending the Gurkhas on future operations.

NOTT: I agree that point and, as an ex-Gurkha, I would, of course, be mortified if we spoilt their chances.

BRAMALL: Look, Secretary of State, I am the Colonel of your Regiment (the 2nd Gurkhas) and I am telling you that they must go and I am requiring your support to fight our corner with the Foreign Office.

NOTT: If you are instructing me in your capacity as Colonel of the 2nd Gurkhas, then of course, Dwin, I have no option but to obey!

So the matter was settled without more ado. My devil's advocacy had been heard and rightly rejected out of hand. Dwin Bramall was correct to call rank.

Dwin later told me that he saw the Prime Minister, told her that he was sending a Gurkha battalion and hoped that was no problem?

'Oh no,' she said, 'why only one?'

The other issues which occupied much of Dwin's time as Chief of Defence Staff and thereafter was what he described as the Fifth Pillar of Defence Policy. We had always regarded the four key elements of defence as being our presence in Germany as part of NATO's land defence of Europe; our naval contribution in the North Atlantic; our Nuclear Deterrent; and Home Defence. No special financial or policy planning had concentrated on our contribution to what was then called our 'out of area' commitments, for instance our presence in the Falklands and Belize, including the substantial training and other help that we gave to our chosen friends worldwide. In fact, we had scarcely enough money to support the Four Pillars described above, let alone an additional Fifth.

Dwin quite fairly expresses the view that the Falklands episode showed up the inadequacy of our planning for 'out of area' crises; we had no choice but to rustle up a policy and a Task Force to meet such an unexpected and unplanned emergency; it had to be done out of the force complement within the Four Pillars.

He suggests that my Defence Review would have diminished our ability to pursue his Fifth Pillar ambitions. Possibly so, but where was the money coming from? He tried to engage Michael Heseltine and the civil servants in his proposals but, while agreeing with them in principle, there was not much enthusiasm so far as I can judge. Heseltine was engaged in his military reorganization – and planning his personal fight against the nuclear protesters. So I think Dwin was frustrated by the unwillingness of the Whitehall machine to engage with his proposal more seriously. It is an uphill struggle to get Whitehall diverted from the status quo and immediate day-to-day crisis management.

In principle, Dwin's idea to bring Foreign Office, MI6 and Ministry of Defence planning more closely together was right. If he felt exasperated at limited progress, he was merely suffering what most Ministers often felt about getting anything positive out of the Whitehall machine. Perhaps the Fifth Pillar is financed and working well. I hope so.

Dwin was always critical of my concentration on European Defence. He always favoured a broad-based Army to meet any worldwide contingency, responding to our global responsibilities. I don't like ambitions unsupported by the resources to meet them. 'Punching above our weight' is a nonsense in my view.

Finally, I come to Dwin's experience at the hands of the police. It was disgraceful. I hope he is remembered as a brave officer and a very distinguished general, especially, as I have said, as a military thinker and historian. But in the immediate future everyone will remember and admire his staunch and utterly brave behaviour in the face of an outrageous series of accusations.

Sir Richard Henriques, a retired High Court Judge, was asked to examine the case and reported forty areas of concern. As a result of false allegations from a single source, the police raided the homes of Lord Bramall, Lord (Leon) Brittan and Harvey Proctor. Suffice it to say, no evidence was found and the Commissioner was forced to pay damages and apologise to Lord Bramall and Diana Brittan.

The former Commissioner of the Metropolitan Police, Sir Bernard Hogan-Howe, who oversaw Operation Midland, as it was called, was rewarded by 'promotion', if that's the word, to the House of Lords. This says two things. First, that the House of Lords in its present state has become an increasingly irrelevant institution, and second, that the police are in dire need of an 'officer class'; a statement made not by me but by Lord Whitelaw when he was Home Secretary. Commissioner Cressida Dick looks like a great improvement in that respect.

When Dwin retired he was an active member of the Lords, President of MCC and Chairman of the Imperial War Museum. I wish him well. He is a very delightful and remarkable person.

Chapter Twenty

Nigel Farage

Politician, broadcaster

I first met Nigel Farage around 1997 at a small dinner party in the London flat of Stuart Wheeler, when he, Rodney Leach and I were battling against our entry into the euro; at that time the euro was enthusiastically supported by the Prime Minister, Tony Blair, the CBI and other obsessive Europhiles like Michael Heseltine and Kenneth Clarke. I was not impressed by Nigel Farage at this first meeting; he talked a lot, and I could not help comparing him with Wheeler and Leach, each of them rather exceptional men. I must therefore mention them before I write about Nigel, whom I admire for his achievement in bringing about a referendum on our membership of the European Union.

Stuart Wheeler made his fortune when he established the spread-betting firm IG Index, and effectively entered politics when he sold his stake for an alleged £70 million. He became the largest donor to the Conservative Party when, on a whim, he gave the Party £5 million when it was in financial straits. Seeing that David Cameron was ambivalent about our membership of the European Union, he later made a donation of £100,000 to UKIP. Cameron, in a foolish gesture, asked for his resignation from the Conservative Party – an act of ill-considered self-harm.

Rodney Leach, later recommended for a peerage as Lord Leach of Fairford, was brilliant academically. He gained a Double First in Greats at Oxford, where he met Jacob Rothschild, and subsequently joined Rothschild as a corporate financier. I met him first in the City when I was a corporate financier at Warburgs.

Rodney's fame came when he founded and became the chairman of Business for Sterling, dedicated to fighting against our entry into the euro. It played an important part in convincing the Chancellor, Gordon Brown, to oppose Tony Blair's enthusiasm for it. Business for Sterling was a huge success in rallying business against the euro – and against that foolish organization the CBI. I have learned over fifty years that I should oppose any proposal that has the support of the CBI; it is a corporatist organisation not a capitalist one.

My next encounter with Nigel Farage was when I attended the by-election in Rochester in 2014; I did so out of curiosity. I have never been a member of UKIP, but I was quite keen, in my wish to force a Referendum on our continuing membership of the European Union, that the UKIP candidate, Mark Reckless, should do well enough to put the frighteners on Cameron.

I think that the UKIP victory in Rochester, together with the remarkable victory of UKIP in the 2014 European Elections, when it came first and gained 28 per cent of the entire national vote, must have convinced David Cameron that he could not hold the Tory vote together in a General Election unless he promised his supporters a vote for a Referendum. And so it came to pass. I shall always support the Conservative Party so long as it stands firm against the Europhile liberal-minded metropolitan classes of our country. We need them in our tent as long as they do not dictate our policies. I think liberals have been a disaster for the cohesion of our society – and Cameron should never have gone into a coalition with the Liberal Party. He should have formed a minority government.

My decision to include a chapter in this book on Nigel Farage was triggered by the apparent refusal of the so-called independent committee for awards to recognize his remarkable achievement. I referred to it in my chapter on David Omand. I cannot put it better than did that maverick journalist Rod Liddle, who wrote in the *Spectator* in July 2016:

> Farage is the most important British politician of the last decade and the most successful. His resignation [as Chairman of UKIP] leaves a hole in our political system. With enormous intelligence and chutzpah and a refreshingly unorthodox approach, he built UKIP up from nothing to become established as our third largest party and succeeded in his overriding ambition – to see the UK vote to leave the European Union.

I agree with Rod Liddle's judgement. I am quite shocked that my recognition of Farage's achievement is detested by so many people. Why is it not possible for people to recognize an achievement even if they are deeply unhappy about the outcome?

I believe that Nigel Farage will be remembered long after Prime Ministers Major, Cameron and May are forgotten – and that is not to diminish their contribution to our democracy. Prime Ministers come and go, seldom causing any change in direction like those brought about by Attlee and Thatcher. Nigel Farage caused such a change in direction, and I think it has been for the good of the country.

Nigel started his professional life as a trader in the City of London. Traders, in my own experience, are not like other businessmen: they have the strength of character to take large risks and show considerable moral courage in carrying their losses when things go wrong. I employed several inveterate traders in Lazard, and they generally made good profits. I tried to persuade my colleagues in our bank not to fill it with Eton-educated Oxbridge graduates with First Class Honours degrees, but to leaven our recruitment with a few brash young traders from the Essex marshes. It would have done us a world of good. Traders are not easy to handle. We had several trading activities in Lazard, in oil, warrants, securities and debt. In my City experience the trading culture in the financial world breeds men and women with rather aggressive personal behaviour, great personal independence and a total lack of loyalty to their employer; they are a mobile community, not unlike the masons of medieval times who could take their skills from one cathedral to another. It was well said of traders: 'If you want loyalty, hire a cocker spaniel.'

I do think that Nigel's twenty years in the London metal exchange as a trader marked his personality and attitudes. I like traders, but they are an awkward, maverick lot! Exactly – that is the core explanation of Nigel Farage's behaviour: energy, determination and a preparedness to take risks. He is a 'lad', 'a cheeky chappie', typical of the rumbustious, outspoken, heavy drinking community of which he was a part.

Although Nigel failed to break the stranglehold of the two main parties when he stood for the parliamentary seat of Thanet, the UKIP bandwagon trundled on in the slipstream of its astonishing victory in the European Election in 2014. But by the time it had achieved its principal objective of forcing a Referendum, it had run out of steam. You cannot expect your supporters who have won a great victory just to pack up their bags and disappear. The problems of UKIP began when it ceased to be a one-issue party. When it filled a gaping hole in our political firmament, it had occupied ground that the main political parties had tried to ignore. Once it sought to broaden out its politics, and to challenge the political consensus, it had only one choice and that was to establish itself as an anti-establishment party confronting both left and right. It could have worked; after all, once Thatcher had been elected in 1979 the Tory Party became a strong radical and anti-establishment party that appealed to a wide section of the country, particularly to the aspiring working class.

Before seeing him again I listened to Nigel's broadcasts on LBC, where he has become a regular commentator. I recommend them. The quality and knowledge of the contributors is outstanding and they have far more scope to give their opinions than in failing BBC programmes like *Question Time*. I am glad he has found a new environment for his talents, which are considerable.

I gave him lunch in my local pub and welcomed him as a leading member of the British establishment! We laughed. I had taken the trouble to do my homework, had read his books and learned about his background, his story and prejudices. He took me through the lot! Oh, how he talked! He has the successful politician's ego, and in spades.

He owed his fame, he said, to his many appearances on YouTube, particularly his speeches in the European Parliament. But more so to his dedication to social media, which he feeds continuously. He claimed he had over two million faithful followers on Twitter and Facebook. He thought that Jeremy Corbyn came next, with something approaching two-thirds of his followers, and Boris Johnson came a long way behind with half a million. Maybe it is an exercise in populism, but it is the new politics. It is frightening how backward the Conservative Party has become when it comes to dominating social media; indeed, social media played a major part in winning the 'Leave' vote in the Referendum, against everything that Cameron and Osborne threw at it, including the then President of the United States, the International Monetary Fund and endless false economic forecasts from the British Treasury.

The problem with Nigel is that he could never lead a party successfully in our democracy. He understands very well the issues that trouble working-class voters, like immigration. But he cannot accept that government in a democracy has to be 'the art of the possible'. Compromise is a necessary element in a democracy if it is to be nurtured and advanced.

His sympathy with authoritarianism has led him to comment favourably on strong men in politics like Putin, and now President Trump. A caller on LBC recently accused him of being a 'propagandist' for Trump. And so he is. There is no denying that Trump's assault on Washington's political class is popular – and his bullying approach to foreign policy could meet with some success. But to imperil the post-war consensus on international trade is a dangerous folly. Trump's tweeting as a mechanism for bypassing a corrupt media may have its purpose, but it is not conducive to considered policymaking and stable government. He is an erratic President, but we have no option but to get along with him. Do I feel safe with the President of the United States? No.

I told Nigel that fewer than half the people in my book would have voted 'Leave'. Most of them achieved positions of power and influence and will fight to retain their privileges; they comprise a well-educated 'mobile elite' of left and right who can take their business, their relations and their networks from place to place, unlike working-class voters in much of the country outside London. This mobile elite is sympathetic to the freedom of movement within the European Union and hostile to the nationalistic sentiments of ordinary people. For the elite the European Union represents enlightened universalism against local chauvinism and it views with alarm the rise of 'populist politicians like you, Nigel' (I said), who claim to speak for the people against the political class. For them, the European Union raises politics above sentimentality and economics.

Nigel and I agreed that if we accept our European identity this should not involve turning our backs on the nation state. Nationality is one of Europe's achievements. It is on the experience of nationality that the European Union *might* have been constructed, a Europe of sovereign nation states in which powers conferred on central institutions could be freely regained. This version inspired the foreign policy of Charles de Gaulle, but it was not accepted by the architects of the European Union, as we know it – however, nationality is at the heart of Europe as a civilisation, a culture and an ideal.

We agreed that the result of the Referendum marks an important turning point in British politics. Nothing like seventeen million people had ever voted for a single political party. For such people something was at stake that had been systematically ignored by politicians, and what was more important to them than all the economic and political arguments was the question of *identity* – 'who are *we*, where are *we* and what holds us together in a shared political order?' I owe these thoughts and this language to the philosopher Roger Scruton, expressed in his 2017 book, *Where We Are: The State of Britain Now*.

The vote did not represent a division between established political parties or ideologies; nor was it a division between regions or social classes. It was a protest by the electorate that when they voted for one of the two main parties at General Elections their choice gave them no opportunity to express their opinions outside a box of policies chosen by a political elite whom they did not respect.

The most obvious example was opinion on the European Union, established as a separate 'nation' in the Maastricht Treaty. Seventeen million people could express their identity through the English nation, but they felt lost – they could not identify themselves within a committee of twenty-eight nations, with an unelected bureaucracy and a politically motivated European Court of Justice.

This vacuum in representative democracy led to the astonishing growth of protest parties, especially UKIP, which grew from nowhere. It has also led to growing rebellion inside Europe, in some countries, against the prison of a eurocurrency dictated by German interests, and in others by a desire for more sovereignty among the countries of the so-called Visegrád Group – the Czech Republic, Hungary, Poland and Slovakia – only recently freed from Communism.

We then discussed Germany and agreed that the country lost its traditional sense of identity through unification in the mid-nineteenth century. Indeed, the trauma of its Nazi past leads it to shelter within the European Union, where it can exercise sovereignty of a different kind, sovereignty over Europe as a whole. Ever since the unification of Germany in the nineteenth century, Germany has fallen under Prussian influences and attitudes. Berlin is predominant.

For several generations since German unification Europe has suffered from 'the German problem', and it has not gone away. Fortunately it is no longer a military problem, but the Germans do not change. Now Germany is using the euro currency to dominate Europe by economic means.

The parity of the euro hugely benefits Germany at the expense of the Mediterranean countries, and even France. Angela Merkel repeatedly defends the euro by saying that the Latin countries must improve their competitiveness, while the best – and indeed the only – way for them to do so is to ditch the euro.

It would be possible for Germany to raise its parity within the euro – or leave the euro temporarily to return at a higher level. It refuses to do so as it would lose its competitiveness and present economic power. The defeated Benelux countries and France still live in fear of Germany and ultimately are subject to its persuasive power and influence.

More seriously, because Germany is the dominant power, the European Commission behaves as if it is under Germany's control. Germany does not contribute its fair share to the defence of Europe through its contribution to the cost of NATO – and it is making itself vulnerable to blackmail by importing over 60 per cent of its energy requirements from Russia. Evidence exists that the Commission has recoiled from bringing Germany to heel for market manipulation, contrary to EU rules.

At present there is not much the British can do about it. We are not strong enough to tackle the German problem. Margaret Thatcher failed to do so when West and East Germany joined together. Inevitably we will be sucked back into Europe at some future date, as we have been twice in the past century. But not now.

Fortunately, thanks to Gordon Brown, we are not members of the Eurozone, and attempts to change the direction of Europe back towards an alliance of nation states have failed. Cameron's negotiation before the Referendum was a humiliation. We are better out of it, to make our own way in the world divorced from the restrictive control of Brussels and EU majority voting. I write as an ex-Trade Secretary hopelessly curbed, as I was, in advancing Great Britain's interests in the wider world.

So how do I sum up my acquaintance with Nigel Farage? I applaud his campaign against the Commission of the European Union – and his long fight for the Referendum. I think that he's an achiever, and I like achievers in business and politics.

The main charge against him among passionate 'Remainers' is that he won – and they have lost. The charge by liberals that he is a 'racist' because he thinks all elected sovereign governments should have control over immigration is clearly absurd.

Personally, I find Farage an interesting man. I do not agree with his approach to politics, which is dogmatic and authoritarian, but as a man of achievement I applaud him without reservation.

Finally, I told Nigel that I voted in favour of our entry into the Common Market in 1967. It was a mistake. I should have listened to Enoch Powell, with whom I started this book, who understood better than I did the consequences that would flow from the Treaty of Rome.

Postscript

I wrote this book of sketches in July of this year before the political scene in the United Kingdom descended into what President Trump has unhelpfully described as 'turmoil'. I expect that he was encouraged by Farage to make this statement. I do not expect the problems for Theresa May to go away before the end of this calendar year. In the meantime the political situation is changing from day to day, and month to month.

The turmoil began with a meeting of the Cabinet at Chequers on 7 July, when the Prime Minister dragooned her colleagues into accepting a compromise plan which has subsequently been published in a White Paper; it certainly overrides several of the Red Lines which she herself laid down in her speeches at Lancaster House, in Florence and elsewhere.

I think it is appropriate to try to find a pathway between the so-called Leavers, characterized at the extreme by Farage, and the Remainers, whose foremost proponent is Philip Hammond, the Chancellor of the Exchequer, who is a captive of the business lobby.

The Prime Minister has abandoned some of her former political colleagues like David Davis, former Secretary of State for Exiting the European Union, preferring to take advice from the civil service, especially Mr Olly Robbins of the Cabinet Office who has been allowed to negotiate with the Commission, thus bypassing Davis's ex-department – which May herself created. It is a mess.

One is bound to say that for all her talents the Prime Minister seems to feel the need for close personal advisers like Nick Timothy and now Olly Robbins, who lead her into serious political trouble. Only politicians can untangle the present political impasse if Theresa May is to survive and carry through the mandate given to the government in the Referendum and overwhelmingly endorsed by Parliament.

Otherwise neutral observers might well ask, is the Prime Minister not leading us into the worst of all worlds, not in the European Union with a voice, but half in it with no voice at all?

As for Project Fear, the propaganda device favoured by the Treasury, it is all nonsense. It is about the Treasury's institutional arrogance, no more. I remember the predictions of chaos with the Millennium Bug and the abolition of Exchange Control; both passed happily, as it will if we leave the European Union. Of course there will be some disruption, but it will be quickly overcome. The British people need to recapture a spirit of adventure; it cannot be achieved as part of a European bureaucracy.

Unless the policies in the White Paper are changed, I fear for the cohesion and prospects of the Conservative Party. It could lead inexorably to a revival of UKIP under Nigel Farage. He looked finished as a politician six months ago; now I am not so sure.

Acknowledgements

Richard Collins has edited several of my books – and I am most grateful to him for his patient work, and friendship.

Penny Cooper has struggled with my poor handwriting and has organized several of my books. I am grateful to her for her painstaking work.

I have had access to several books, biographies and letters about the people whom I have encountered in my life, not least:

Jonathan Aitken, *Margaret Thatcher: Power and Personality*, Bloomsbury Continuum, 2014

Richard Hill, *Lewin of Greenwich: The Authorised Biography of Admiral of the Fleet Lord Lewin*, Cassell, 2000

Simon Heffer, *Like the Roman: The Life of Enoch Powell*, Cassell, 2008

Michael Crick, *Michael Heseltine: A Biography*, Hamish Hamilton, 1997

Martin Rees, *Our Final Century: Will the Human Race Survive the Twenty-First Century?*, Heinemann, 2003

Michael Tillotson, *Dwin Bramall: The Authorised Biography of Field Marshal the Lord Bramall KG, GCB, OBE, MC*, History Press, 2013

Bill Jackson and Dwin Bramall, *The Chiefs: The Story of the United Kingdom Chiefs of Staff*, Brassey's, 1992

Ted Hughes, *Tales from Ovid*, 1997, and *Birthday Letters*, 1998, both published by Faber & Faber

I found it a real pleasure dealing with the editorial staff at Pen & Sword in Barnsley including Henry Wilson, the commissioning editor. Finally, I must thank my son-in-law Sir Hugo Swire MP, whose idea it was to publish this book – and Bernard Kelly, who has generously allowed me to share his office in the King's Road, and to whom I owe a great deal.

I have known all the people in these 'encounters', either recently or before their decease, and I am most grateful to them for allowing me, where possible, to include them in this book.